THE Faith of Jesus

THE Faith of Jesus

A Christian doctrine course based on the teachings of our Lord Jesus Christ, according to the holy Scriptures.

Carlos A. Aeschlimann

Nampa, Idaho | www.pacificpress.com

Cover design by Gerald Lee Monks
Cover design resources from iStockphoto.com

To order additional copies of this book, call toll-free 1-800-765-6955, or visit AdventistBookCenter.com.

ISBN 978-0-8163-6593-7

November 2024

Contents

What the Bible Teaches About

ITS OWN VALUE

REVEALED BY GOD

1. Who revealed the holy Scriptures? 2 Timothy 3:16

____

2. Who received the revelation? Hebrews 1:1

____

SOURCE OF GUIDANCE AND SOLUTIONS

3. The holy Bible is compared to what? Psalm 119:105

____

4. What benefit does one receive from studying the Bible? 2 Timothy 3:15–17

____

5. What blessings does the holy Bible offer? Romans 15:4

____

6. How long will the Bible endure? Isaiah 40:8

____

WHAT MUST I DO?

7. Read your Bible every day (Deuteronomy 17:19).
8. Study it regularly (John 5:39).
9. Accept it with joy and gladness (Jeremiah 15:16).
10. Practice its teachings (Revelation 1:3).

I believe that the holy Bible is inspired by God. I accept it as my rule of faith. I promise to read it daily.

____

SIGNATURE

ADDITIONAL STUDY

The Bible is the source of truth. (John 17:17; Isaiah 8:20). It was inspired by God and the Holy Spirit (2 Peter 1:19–21; 2 Samuel 23:2). Therefore, we must not reject its teachings (1 Samuel 15:23).

The Bible has power to transform lives. (Hebrews 4:12). It produces rebirth and spiritual growth (1 Peter 1:23; 2:2).

The Bible contains remarkable scientific facts. The earth hangs on nothing (Job 26:7). Air has weight (Job 28:25). The number of stars is incalculable (Jeremiah 33:22).

The Bible must be studied and obeyed. We are invited to study the Bible (John 5:24, 39; Isaiah 28:13). We must obey its counsel (John 14:23). By reading it, we are participants of the divine nature (2 Peter 1:4).

What is the Bible?

The Bible is the holy Book of the Christian. It also is called the holy Scriptures. It is the most precious jewel of Western thought and culture. More than that, it is the revelation of God to man.

Actually, the Bible is a collection of books. It contains sixty-six books in two "testaments." The Old Testament was written before Christ, and the New Testament is the story of Christ and the development of Christianity. The Bible was written over a period spanning fifteen hundred years by about forty authors, including wise men, kings, shepherds, farmers, doctors, and lawmakers.

The opinion of great men

Emilio Castellar, a famous Spanish writer and politician, said: "The Bible is the purest revelation that shows God exists." Emmanuel Kant, a famous German philosopher, said: "The existence of the Bible, as a book for the people, is the greatest benefit that the human race has ever experienced." Count Leo Tolstoy, a prominent Russian writer, said: "The moral development of man and child is impossible without reading the Bible."

Advice about studying the Bible

Every Christian should own and study the holy Book of God. Jesus said, "Search the scriptures" (John 5:39). Jerome, the translator of the version of the Bible called the Latin Vulgate, said: "We must cultivate intelligence through the reading of the holy books."

Cardinal Garibi Rivera, the former archbishop of Guadalajara, said: "If the faithful propose to read Scripture regularly, they will have a deeper understanding of the divine Revelation, taken from the written Word of God. Prayer on the one hand, and reading the Bible on the other, are a Christian conversation with God, used to nourish your spiritual life." The second Vatican council said this about the Bible: "The Church has always venerated the divine Scriptures. . . . This sacred synod earnestly and especially urges all the Christian faithful, too, especially religious, to learn by frequent reading of the divine Scriptures the 'excelling knowledge of Jesus Christ' (Phil. 3:8)."[1]

Illustrations

An ancient Roman legend says that a young man named Fortunato possessed a magic bag that contained a single gold coin, which miraculously renewed itself each time he took it out and spent it because the currency had the rare virtue of always returning to the bag. The holy Bible is similar because we are enriched by its teachings as we open its pages. Then we close it, and when we open it again, we find the same riches. The Bible always has untold treasures of advice and guidance.

What the Bible Teaches About

THE EXISTENCE OF GOD

2

GOD

1. How many gods are there? Ephesians 4:6

____

2. What is the nature of God? John 4:24

____

3. Who are the Three Persons of the Trinity? Matthew 28:19

____

4. What is God's character like? 1 John 4:8

____

GOD AND MAN

5. How does God consider Himself toward man? 1 John 3:1, 2

____

6. Does God care about our problems? Psalm 40:1–3

____

WHAT MUST I DO?

1. Respect the name of God (Exodus 20:7).
2. Obey God (Acts 5:29).
3. Put God in first place (Matthew 6:33).
4. Love God with all your heart (Matthew 22:37).

I believe in God the Father, Jesus the Son, and the Holy Spirit.
I promise to love and obey Him as my heavenly Father.

____

SIGNATURE

ADDITIONAL STUDY

We believe in only one God (1 Corinthians 8:6). God is manifested in three persons (Matthew 28:19).

God is the Creator of the universe (Genesis 1:1; Isaiah 45:18; Hebrews 1:10).

What is God like? He is immortal (1 Timothy 6:16). He is spirit (John 4:24). He is eternal (Isaiah 57:15). He is love (1 John 4:8).

God reveals himself in nature (Psalm 19:1), in the Bible (Revelation 1:1), and in the Lord Jesus (John 14:6).

God is our Father. He worries about our problems (Psalm 46:1). He supports us with mercy (Jeremiah 31:3). He comforts us in our pain (2 Corinthians 1:3, 4). He supplies all we are lacking (Philippians 4:19).

Our attitude toward God. We must trust in Him (Psalm 52:8) and keep His commandments (Ecclesiastes 12:13). If we obey Him, things will go well for us (Romans 8:28).

The need for God

Humanity's hardships and sufferings are the result of its separation from God. The prophet Jeremiah speaks about this terrible error: "For my people have committed two evils; they have forsaken me the fountain of living waters, and hewed them out cisterns, broken cisterns, that can hold no water" (Jeremiah 2:13).

The only solution is to return to God. Doctor Andrew Conway Ivy, renowned professor from the University of Illinois, said: "Belief in the existence of God provides the only complete, ultimate and rational meaning to existence."[2]

Philosopher Will Durant adds: "The greatest question of our time is not communism vs. individualism, not Europe vs. America, not even the East vs. the West; it is whether men can bear to live without God."[3]

The wonderful thing is that as soon as we take one step toward God, we will find that He is waiting for us with love and mercy (Ephesians 2:4, 5).

The existence of God

Some say: "I do not believe in God because I do not see him." However, there are many things we believe in without seeing. For example, electricity, wind, and love. Others say; "I do not believe because I do not understand God."

Who does not believe in God? "The fool hath said in his heart, There is no God" (Psalm 14:1). What do men of science say about God? Sir Isaac Newton, famous for discovering the universal law of gravity, stated: "This most beautiful System of the Sun, Planets, and Comets, could only proceed from the counsel and dominion of an intelligent powerful being."[4]

Therefore God is in fact a divine, wise, and omnipotent God, a Being that is above all things and infinitely wise.

Trust in God

Dr. Wernher Von Braun, inventor of interplanetary rockets, said: "Our need for God is not just based on awe alone. Man needs faith just as he needs food, water, or air."[5]

In the Bible, there are wonderful promises for those who trust in God: "All things work together for good to them that love God" (Romans 8:28). "If God be for us, who can be against us?" (Romans 8:31). God can supply all our needs (Philippians 4:19).

What must we do for God to be with us and protect us? Yearn wholeheartedly for God (Psalm 42:1). Obey God and keep His commandments (Ecclesiastes 12:13). Put God above all things (Matthew 6:33). Love Him with all our heart (Matthew 22:37).

What the Bible Teaches About

THE HOLY SPIRIT 3

THE PERSONALITY OF THE HOLY SPIRIT

1. Besides the Holy Spirit, who forms part of the Godhead? Matthew 28:19

   ____

2. Who sends the Holy Spirit, and what is He called? John 15:26

   ____

THE WORK OF THE HOLY SPIRIT

3. The Holy Spirit guides us to what? John 16:13

   ____

4. The Holy Spirit convicts us of what? John 16:8–11

   ____

5. What assurance does the Holy Spirit give us? Romans 8:14, 16, 17

   ____

6. How long will the Holy Spirit be with the faithful? John 14:16

   ____

RECEIVING THE HOLY SPIRIT

7. What is the condition for receiving the Holy Spirit? Acts 5:32

   ____

8. What is the fruit of the Holy Spirit? Galatians 5:22–26

   ____

WHAT MUST I DO?

1. Do not grieve Him (Ephesians 4:30).
2. Do not blaspheme or speak against the Holy Spirit (Matthew 12:31, 32).
3. Ask God for Him (Luke 11:13).

I believe that the Holy Spirit is real, and I desire that He take possession of my life.

____

SIGNATURE

ADDITIONAL STUDY

Other names for the Holy Spirit

- Spirit of Christ (1 Peter 1:11).
- Spirit of truth (John 14:17; 15:26).
- Spirit of God (Exodus 31:3).
- Spirit of Jehovah (1 Samuel 16:14).
- Spirit (Luke 4:1).

The divinity of the Holy Spirit

- He is God (Acts 5:3, 4).
- He is eternal like God (Hebrews 9:14).
- He is omnipotent and omnipresent like God (Psalm 139).
- He is omniscient (1 Corinthians 2:10, 11).
- He is a Creator like God (Job 33:4).

The personality of the Holy Spirit

- Gives gifts (1 Corinthians 12:11).
- Intercedes (Romans 8:26).
- Can be grieved (Ephesians 4:30).
- Speaks (1 Timothy 4:1).
- Has knowledge (1 Corinthians 2:11).
- Teaches (1 Corinthians 2:12).
- Approves (Acts 15:28).
- Bears witness (Romans 8:16).
- Commissions (Acts 13:2).
- Impedes (Acts 16:6, 7).
- Administers, distributes (1 Corinthians 12:1).
- Can be resisted (Acts 7:51).

The functions of the Holy Spirit

- Gives gifts (1 Corinthians 12:7–11).
- Reveals Christ to us (John 16:14).
- Inspires the prophets (2 Samuel 23:2; 2 Peter 1:21).
- Transmits the love of God to human beings (Romans 5:5).
- Is the representative of Christ on earth (John 14:26).
- Dwells in human beings (1 Corinthians 3:16, 17; 6:19, 20).
- Can be sinned against (Matthew 12:31; Hebrews 10:26).

Commentary

"There are three living persons of the heavenly trio."[6]

"The Father is all the fullness of the Godhead bodily, and is invisible to mortal sight. The Son [of God] is all the fullness of the Godhead manifested. . . .

"The Comforter that Christ promised to send after He ascended to heaven, is the Spirit in all the fullness of the Godhead, making manifest the power of divine grace to all who receive and believe in Christ as a personal Saviour."[7]

"God is not a magnified or sublimated man. God alone has perfect personality. His perfect personality has existed since the days of eternity, long before a single human being, with his limitations, came to be. There are four things that are predicated of personality: (1) Will; (2) Intelligence; (3) Power; (4) Capacity for love. Personality involves a self-conscious, self-knowing, self-willing, and self-determining being. A person is therefore a being who is approachable, who can be trusted or doubted, loved or hated, adored or insulted. These essentials of personality are but limited and imperfect in man, but limitless and perfect in God. So the personality of the Holy Spirit is not to be confined to comparisons with man.

"It will help us to listen to Jesus on this point here in these two chapters of John, the fourteenth and sixteenth. Not a word does Jesus utter that can be construed as implying that the Holy Spirit is simply an influence. He addresses Him and treats Him as a person. He calls Him the Paraclete, which is the title of a person. . . .

". . . The Holy Spirit is more than a personality. He is a divine personality. He is called God (Acts 5:3, 4) the 'third person of the Godhead.' "[8]

What the Bible Teaches About

COMMUNICATION WITH GOD 4

PRAYER

1. How do we communicate with God? Daniel 9:3

   ____

2. What is prayer? 1 Samuel 1:9–15

   ____

3. How much power does sincere prayer have? James 5:16

   ____

4. In whose name should we pray? John 14:13

   ____

5. Does God answer prayers? Matthew 7:7–11

   ____

FAITH

6. How is faith described? Hebrews 11:1, 6

   ____

7. How is faith developed? Romans 10:17

   ____

WHAT MUST I DO?

1. Pray three times a day (Psalm 55:17).
2. Practice private prayer (Matthew 6:6).
3. Ask with faith (Matthew 21:22).
4. Ask with correct motives (James 4:3).

I believe that God hears and answers prayers.
I will pray with faith every day.

____

SIGNATURE

ADDITIONAL STUDY

We should pray regularly (Luke 18:1; Romans 12:12). The best plan is to pray three times a day (Daniel 6:10). One must have a spirit of constant prayer (1 Thessalonians 5:17).

What to pray about: Gratitude (Philippians 4:6). Various petitions (James 1:5; John 15:7). Confession of sin (Daniel 9:20; Psalm 32:3–6). The needs of others (Job 42:10).

Conditions for God to answer prayers: Ask with faith (Matthew 21:22). Ask well (James 4:3). Ask according to God's will (Luke 22:41, 42). Manifest a forgiving spirit (Mark 11:25). Be perseverant (Luke 18:1). Keep the commandments (1 John 3:22).

Obstacles that keep God from answering: Asking selfishly (James 4:3). Doubts (James 1:6). Lack of a forgiving spirit (Matthew 6:14, 15). Sin cherished in the heart (Psalm 66:18). Disobedience to God's holy law (Proverbs 28:9).

God promises to answer prayers. (Psalm 3:4; 40:1, 2; Matthew 7:7–12).

What is prayer?

"Prayer is the opening of the heart to God as to a friend.

". . . Prayer is the key in the hand of faith to unlock heaven's storehouse, where are treasured the boundless resources of Omnipotence."[9]

Types of prayer

Some prayers consist of reciting a prayer that is already written. The most famous of these is the Lord's Prayer, given by Jesus. Prayer is speaking to God with our own words to tell Him the needs that afflict us.

There are several types of prayer. Public prayer is for collective matters. In family prayer, the problems of the home are mentioned. Prayer for a meal is for thanking God for the meal and asking for His blessing (Luke 24:30; 22:19). The most beneficial prayer for the soul is private prayer.

There is also mental prayer, which is prayed without using audible words.

Parts of the prayer

You begin by saying: "Our Father" (Matthew 6:9), and then continue with what you desire to say to or ask from God. You end in Jesus' name (John 16:23) and with the word "amen," which means "so be it."

The wonderful effects of prayer

The famous physician Alexis Carrel stated: "Prayer is the most powerful form of energy that one can generate. . . .

"Prayer is a force as real as terrestrial gravity. As a physician, I have seen men, after all other therapy has failed, lifted out of disease and melancholy by the serene effort of prayer."[10]

"Keep your wants, your joys, your sorrows, your cares, and your fears before God [in prayer]. You cannot burden Him; you cannot weary Him. . . . His heart of love is touched by our sorrows and even by our utterances of them. Take to Him everything that perplexes the mind. Nothing is too great for Him to bear. . . . Nothing that in any way concerns our peace is too small for Him to notice. . . . No calamity can befall the least of His children, no anxiety harass the soul, no joy cheer, no sincere prayer escape the lips, of which our heavenly Father is unobservant, or in which He takes no immediate interest."[11]

What the Bible Teaches About

CHRIST'S SECOND COMING

5

JESUS PROMISES TO RETURN

1. What wonderful promise did Jesus make? John 14:1–3

___

2. How should we consider this promise? Titus 2:13

___

HOW JESUS WILL COME

3. In what way will Jesus return? Matthew 24:30

___

4. How many will see His glorious Advent? Revelation 1:7

___

WHY JESUS WILL COME

5. What is the objective of Christ's coming? Matthew 16:27

___

6. What will happen with the righteous dead? 1 Thessalonians 4:13–16

___

7. What will happen with all the righteous? 1 Thessalonians 4:17

___

WHAT MUST I DO?

1. Desire the coming of Jesus (2 Timothy 4:8).
2. Prepare myself to be ready (1 John 3:2, 3).
3. Help with the preaching of the gospel (Matthew 24:14).

I believe in Jesus' second coming. I want to prepare myself to be with Him in heaven.

___

SIGNATURE

ADDITIONAL STUDY

Jesus promises to return

- The promise in the Old Testament: Job 19:25–27; Psalm 96:13; Isaiah 26:21; 40:10; 62:11; 66:15.
- The promise in the New Testament: Matthew 24:30; 16:27; 25:31; 26:64; Philippians 3:20, 21; 1 Corinthians 1:7, 8; 2 Peter 1:16; Hebrews 9:28; Jude 14; Revelation 1:7; 22:12, 20.

How and why will Jesus return?

His coming will be personal and visible (Acts 1:11). All His angels will be with Him (Matthew 25:31). It will be like lightning (Matthew 24:27) and will destroy the wicked (2 Thessalonians 2:8, 9). The righteous will be resurrected, and the living transformed (1 Corinthians 15:51–55).

Attitude at the coming of Jesus

- The wicked will be desperate (Revelation 6:15–17).
- The righteous will rejoice (Isaiah 25:9).
- The believers prepare for the glorious Advent (Matthew 24:42; 2 Peter 3:14; Titus 2:11–14).

A new world of joy

In the new world there will be amazing wonders (1 Corinthians 2:9). Nature will be transformed (Isaiah 11:6–9). There will be no more suffering, sickness, or death (Revelation 21:1–4). We will be with Jesus forever (Revelation 22:1–6).

The blessed hope

One of the wonderful Christian doctrines is the glorious Advent of the Lord Jesus. It is said that the early Christians would greet each other with the word *maranatha*, which means "the Lord is coming."

The Second Advent is a Christian, biblical doctrine. Millions have prayed the Lord's Prayer and have said, "Thy kingdom come." By repeating this, they have declared: "He shall come to judge the living and the dead."

This doctrine is found throughout the Bible. Enoch, the seventh from Adam, prophesied about this extraordinary event. The majority of the Old Testament prophets referred to end-time events and the coming of Jesus. In the New Testament, the events that will take place at the end of the world are an important part of the teachings of Jesus and the apostles. Revelation ends with a poignant plea: "He which testifieth these things saith, Surely I come quickly. Amen. Even so, come, Lord Jesus" (Revelation 22:20).

Testimonies

Christians in general believe in the coming of Jesus. "It is a truth of faith that Jesus Christ will return at end of the world to judge the living and the dead. . . . In that last day all justice shall be completed. Reward will be given even to the last fruits of good works and the latest scandals of the evil deeds of sinners will be punished."[12]

"Strong in faith we look for 'the blessed hope and glorious coming of our great God and Savior, Jesus Christ' (Tit. 2:13) 'who will refashion the body of our lowliness, conforming it to the body of his glory' (Phil. 3:21) and who will come 'to be glorified in his saints, and to be marveled at in all those who have believed' (2 Th. 1:10)."[13]

"The fabulous future that we expect as Christians will not be the natural development of history. . . . It will come in the establishment of the Kingdom of God by God's direct intervention!"[14]

What the Bible Teaches About

THE SIGNS BEFORE CHRIST'S RETURN

6

WHEN WILL HE COME?

1. What did Jesus' disciples ask? Matthew 24:3

____

2. Is the date of Jesus' return known? Matthew 24:36

____

3. Are we in darkness regarding Jesus' coming? 1 Thessalonians 5:1–4

____

SIGNS THAT ANNOUNCE JESUS' RETURN

4. What signs did Jesus predict? Matthew 24:6, 7

____

5. What will be the prevalent social conditions? James 5:1–5

____

6. What will be the moral condition of humanity? 2 Timothy 3:1–5

____

7. What will happen with knowledge? Daniel 12:4

____

8. What signs will be seen in the stars? Matthew 24:29

____

WHAT MUST I DO?

1. Be aware of the signs of the times (Luke 21:28–31).
2. Watch and be prepared (Matthew 24:42, 44).

I believe that Jesus will come very soon. I will prepare myself to be ready and go with Jesus to the new earth.

____

SIGNATURE

ADDITIONAL STUDY

The time of His Advent. We do not know the exact moment of His coming (Matthew 24:42, 44). Determining the time of His coming is something that only God can do (Acts 1:7). His coming will be surprising (Luke 12:40; 21:34), as a thief in the night (2 Peter 3:10; 1 Thessalonians 5:2). But we are not in darkness because Jesus gave unmistakable signs (Matthew 24:33; 1 Thessalonians 5:1–4).

Signs that announce Jesus' return. Rise of immorality (Luke 17:26, 27; Micah 7:1–3). Fear and anguish (Luke 21:25, 26; Matthew 24:21, 22). Natural disasters (Luke 21:11). False Christs (Matthew 24:5, 23, 24). Generalized apostasy (Matthew 24:11; 2 Peter 3:3, 4). Preaching of the gospel worldwide (Matthew 24:14).

Preparation for Jesus' return. Waiting and speeding up our preparation (2 Peter 3:12), we must always be prepared (Luke 12:40). We have to be diligent to be found without spot (2 Peter 3:14). According to the holy Bible, we do not know the exact day nor the hour of Jesus' return. However, just as there were clear prophecies about Jesus' birth, there are clear signs for the Second Advent. The fulfillment of the signs indicates the time of the end and the imminence of Jesus' return.

Cosmic signs

- **Great earthquake**. "And I beheld when he had opened the sixth seal, and, lo, there was a great earthquake; and the sun became black as sackcloth of hair, and the moon became as blood; and the stars of heaven fell unto the earth" (Revelation 6:12, 13). This earthquake happened on November 10, 1755; it destroyed Lisbon and shook Europe and northern Africa.
- **Darkening of the sun**. (Isaiah 24:23; Joel 2:30, 31; Mark 13:24; Matthew 24:29). This extraordinary event happened on May 19, 1780. The day started normally, but by midmorning a strange darkness covered a great part of the United States. The celebrated astronomer Herschel said: "The dark day in Northern America was one of those wonderful phenomena of nature which will always be read with interest, but which philosophy is at a loss to explain."[15]
- **Falling stars**. (Matthew 24:29; Revelation 6:13). This remarkable sign happened on the night of November 13, 1833. An eyewitness said that the stars fell so abundantly that you could read the newspaper by their light.

Knowledge shall be increased

Daniel predicted that in the time of the end, "knowledge shall be increased" (Daniel 12:4). This clear sign is fulfilled dramatically before our eyes. "Human knowledge doubles every fifteen years, and man has gone from the horse cart to missiles in less than two generations."[16]

A glorious dawn approaches

The exact fulfillment of the signs announced by Jesus and the prophets indicates to us that the long and devastating night of pain and death will soon come to an end. We can see glimpses of the radiant dawn of the new world offered by Jesus to "all who love His coming."

What the Bible Teaches About

THE ORIGIN OF SIN AND EVIL

7

THE BEGINNING OF SIN

1. When and where did sin begin? Revelation 12:7–10

____

2. In whom did sin originate? Ezekiel 28:14–17

____

SIN ON EARTH

3. What sign of obedience did God give to Adam and Eve? Genesis 2:15–17

____

4. What did the first sin consist of? Genesis 3:1–6

____

THE TERRIBLE CONSEQUENCES OF SIN

5. What is sin? 1 John 3:4

____

6. Whom does the sinner submit to? 1 John 3:8

____

7. What is the final result of sin? Romans 6:23

____

WHAT MUST I DO?

1. Resist Satan in God's name (James 4:7).
2. Do not compromise with sin (Romans 6:12).
3. Overcome with Jesus' help (Romans 8:37).

I will try, with God's help, to cleanse my life from all sin.

____

SIGNATURE

ADDITIONAL STUDY

Satan (Lucifer) is the author of sin. Lucifer was created perfect (Ezekiel 28:14, 15). He wanted to be equal with God (Isaiah 14:13, 14). A battle took place in heaven (Revelation 12:7–9). Lucifer did not remain in the truth (John 8:44). He sinned from the beginning (1 John 3:8).

What is sin? Sin is the transgression of God's law (1 John 3:4). Every injustice is sin (1 John 5:17). Knowing what is right and not doing it is sin. (James 4:17). Rejecting Jesus' message is sin (John 15:22).

The terrible consequences of sin. Takes away peace from the soul (Isaiah 57:20, 21; Romans 2:9). Separates the person from God (Isaiah 59:2). Turns the sinner into a servant of Satan (1 John 3:8). Causes eternal death (Romans 6:23).

Effective help in the fight against sin. We have a constant battle against the devil's snares (Ephesians 6:11, 12). If we are with God, the devil flees (James 4:7). We have a full armor to defend us from the evil one's attacks (Ephesians 6:11–18). Christ's blood cleanses us from sin (1 John 1:7).

Who created Satan?

God did not create Satan (*adversary*), but rather Lucifer (*bright star*), a creature of extraordinary beauty and intelligence. Little by little, Lucifer began to cultivate envy, hatred, and pride. He desired to be equal to God. He rebelled against God, accusing Him of tyranny and lack of love. God did not destroy Satan in order to allow him to manifest the cruelty of his actions over time so that there would be no doubt about divine love and justice.

Original sin

"So God created man in his own image, in the image of God created he him. . . . And God saw every thing that he had made, and, behold, it was very good" (Genesis 1:27, 31). God gave man intelligence, reasoning, and the capacity to freely choose his destiny.

Confronting Satan and falling into temptation, Adam and Even committed the sin of disobedience to a definite command from God. Also, they exercised their power of choice mistakenly. Eve believed Satan and mistrusted God. In this way, the first couple rejected their Father God and put themselves under Satan's control.

The seriousness of sin

"From the sole of the foot even unto the head, there is no soundness in it; but wounds, and bruises, and putrefying sores: they have not been closed, neither bound up, neither mollified with ointment" (Isaiah 1:6). The prophet compares sin to the terrible sickness called leprosy. God hates sin, but he loves the sinner. He wants to see the sinner free of the horrible consequences.

Sin always causes tragedy and problems. "When I kept silence, my bones waxed old through my roaring all the day long. For day and night thy hand was heavy upon me: my moisture is turned into the drought of summer" (Psalm 32:3, 4). The worst consequences of sin are the destruction of spiritual life and estrangement from God.

The end of sin

The disastrous experience of sin will come to an end along with its author, the devil: Satan and his angels are reserved for the judgment of the great day (Jude 6). Ultimately, they will be destroyed in the great lake of fire (Revelation 20:10). Sin will be eliminated, and it will never again appear (Malachi 4:1).

What the Bible Teaches About

THE GIFT FROM GOD FOR OUR SALVATION

8

THE TERRIBLE CONSEQUENCES OF SIN

1. What is the final consequence of sin? Romans 5:12

   ____

2. Can man resolve the problem of sin? Jeremiah 2:22

   ____

JESUS SAVES THE SINNER

3. What provision did God make to save man? John 3:16

   ____

4. How did Jesus describe His mission? Luke 19:10

   ____

5. Did Jesus commit any sins? Hebrews 4:15

   ____

6. How did Jesus pay for man's debt? Isaiah 53:3–7

   ____

7. What act ensured our salvation? 1 Corinthians 15:20–22

   ____

WHAT MUST I DO?

1. Believe in Jesus (Acts 16:30, 31).
2. Accept Him as my only Savior (Acts 4:12).
3. Open the door of my heart to Him (Revelation 3:20).

I believe that Jesus died for me. I accept Him as my only Savior. I surrender my life and heart to Him.

____

SIGNATURE

ADDITIONAL STUDY

Sin and its terrible consequences. All human beings have sinned (1 John 1:8). The sinner is in servitude to Satan (2 Peter 2:19). The sinner's final fate is death (Romans 6:23). The sinner cannot do anything to save himself (Jeremiah 2:22).

Love's plan. The plan of salvation has always existed (2 Timothy 1:9; Ephesians 3:8, 9).

Jesus is the only Savior. The apostle Peter declared that Jesus is the only Savior (Acts 4:12). How did Jesus save us? Let's look at seven redeeming acts:

1. Incarnation. Jesus, being God, became man (John 1:1–4; Galatians 4:4; Hebrews 2:14).
2. Life without sin (Hebrews 4:14–16; 1 John 3:5; 1 Peter 2:22).
3. Vicarious death (1 Peter 2:24; 1 Timothy 1:15; Romans 5:8).
4. Resurrection (Romans 4:25; 1 Corinthians 15:5, 13, 14).
5. Ascension to heaven (1 Timothy 3:16).
6. Intercession (1 Timothy 2:5; Hebrews 7:25).
7. Advent (Hebrews 9:28).

We are saved by grace. Salvation is freely granted (Romans 3:24; Ephesians 2:8). In order to obtain it, you have to believe in Jesus (Acts 16:30, 31; Hebrews 4:16).

The plan of salvation

If a child falls in a chasm, the parent will do everything possible to get him out. If a child is kidnapped, parents will pay any amount to rescue her. If the child is sick, they will hire the best doctor and buy the most expensive medication. God lost His children. They fell in the chasm of sin. They were kidnapped by Satan. They are sick because of sin. But God, like a good Father, took all measures to save them. The cost of the redemption of humanity was nothing less than the precious blood of Jesus (1 Peter 1:18, 19).

The plan to save man is a plan of love (1 John 3:16). It consisted of God giving His Son (John 3:16). The Son was coming to seek what had been lost (Luke 19:10) and would give His life as the price to rescue the sinner (1 Timothy 2:6).

Jesus, the only sufficient Savior

If we are sick, we can choose any physician and even change doctors. For the disease of sin, there is only one Physician that can save us: Christ. "Neither is there salvation in any other: for there is none other name [besides Christ's] under heaven given among men, whereby we must be saved" (Acts 4:12).

Freely saved by God's grace

No treasure could pay for the indescribable gift of salvation. That is why God grants salvation freely. "In whom we have redemption through his blood, the forgiveness of sins, according to the riches of his grace" (Ephesians 1:7). "For by grace are ye saved through faith; and that not of yourselves: it is the gift of God" (Ephesians 2:8). But we must believe in Jesus and have faith in His power to save us (Acts 16:31; Romans 5:1).

The end of sin

Neither root nor branch of sin will remain (Malachi 4:1). The earth shall be purified (2 Peter 3:10). All things will be made new (Revelation 21:5). There shall be no more curse or sin (Revelation 22:3).

Quotes about salvation

"We believe that the Father so loved the world that He gave His own Son to save it. Indeed, through this same Son of His He freed us from bondage to sin." "Christ . . . is the one Mediator and the unique Way of salvation."[17]

"The heart of God yearns over His earthly children with a love stronger than death. In giving up His Son, He has poured out to us all heaven in one gift. The Saviour's life and death and intercession, the ministry of angels, the pleading of the Spirit, the Father working above and through all, the unceasing interest of heavenly beings,—all are enlisted in behalf of man's redemption."[18]

What the Bible Teaches About

THE FORGIVENESS OF OUR SINS

9

THE ONLY WAY TO SALVATION

1. Thanks to whom and what are we saved? 1 Peter 2:24

   ____

2. How much does salvation cost? Romans 3:24

   ____

OBTAINING FORGIVENESS

3. What does the sinner need to recognize sincerely? Luke 18:10–14

   ____

4. What deep feeling is indispensable? Acts 2:37, 38

   ____

5. What must be done with sins? Psalm 32:3–5

   ____

THE SWEET CERTAINTY OF FORGIVENESS

6. What marvelous offer does God make? Isaiah 1:18

   ____

7. How complete is divine forgiveness? Isaiah 43:25

   ____

WHAT MUST I DO?

1. Repent with all my heart (Acts 3:19).
2. Confess all my sin (1 John 1:9).
3. Experience conversion (Ezekiel 36:25–27).

I ask forgiveness for my sins. I believe that God will forgive me. I want to live a holy life in Jesus.

____

SIGNATURE

ADDITIONAL STUDY

Steps for obtaining forgiveness:

1. Recognizing the condition of the sinner (1 John 1:8; Psalm 51:2, 3).
2. Sincere repentance (Acts 3:19; Luke 3:8; 13:3–5).
3. Accepting Jesus as the only Savior (Acts 4:12; 5:31; 10:43).
4. Confession. Confession is indispensable (Psalm 32:1–5; Proverbs 28:13). Must name the sin that was committed (Leviticus 5:5). Will pay for the damages caused (Leviticus 6:4). Confession must be made to God (1 John 1:9; Isaiah 1:18; Psalm 103:3).
5. Conversion (2 Chronicles 7:14; Acts 3:19).

God's marvelous forgiveness

God forgives completely (Isaiah 43:25; Hebrews 8:12; 10:17). Forgiveness is free (Romans 3:24). We are forgiven in the act (Luke 23:39–43). Obtaining forgiveness is like bringing an account current. The sinner does not have something to pay the debt with, but Jesus paid for him on the cross at Calvary and offers the merits of His sacrifice to whoever wishes to accept them.

Forgiveness

True repentance consists of sincere and deep pain for having sinned (2 Corinthians 7:10). Repentance is indispensable for obtaining forgiveness (Acts 2:37, 38).

Confession

Sins must be declared to God; only He can forgive them. There cannot be forgiveness without sincere, complete confession (Proverbs 28:13). "Confession of sin, whether public or private, should be heartfelt and freely expressed. It is not to be urged from the sinner. It is not to be made in a flippant and careless way. . . . Confession will not be acceptable to God without sincere repentance and reformation. There must be decided changes in the life; everything offensive to God must be put away. This will be the result of genuine sorrow for sin."[19]

Conversion

As a direct result of repentance and confession, a radical change happens in the sinner's character. "Therefore if any man be in Christ, he is a new creature: old things are passed away; behold, all things are become new" (2 Corinthians 5:17).

"Those who become new creatures in Christ Jesus will bring forth the fruits of the spirit, 'love, joy, peace, long-suffering, gentleness, goodness, faith, meekness, temperance.' Galatians 5:22, 23. They will no longer fashion themselves according to the former lusts, but by the faith of the Son of God they will follow in his steps, reflect his character, and purify themselves even as he is pure. The things they once hated they now love, and the things they once loved they hate. The proud and self-assertive become meek and lowly in heart. The vain and supercilious become serious and unobtrusive. The drunken become sober, and the profligate pure."[20]

Justification

"Therefore being justified by faith, we have peace with God through our Lord Jesus Christ. . . . For when we were yet without strength, in due time Christ died for the ungodly. . . . But God commendeth his love toward us, in that, while we were yet sinners, Christ died for us. Much more then, being now justified by his blood, we shall be saved from wrath through him" (Romans 5:1–9).

"God's forgiveness goes much farther than the forgiveness of sin. God not only forgives, He justifies. This means that man is actually without guilt in God's sight."[21]

Sanctification

After justification, and with God's help, we must maintain ourselves without falling (Jude 24). There should not be voluntary sin (Hebrews 10:26). The secret of sanctification is to grow in the knowledge of God (Colossians 1:10). The only way to have this experience of continuous progress is to be intimately connected to Jesus and to trust in His power (Galatians 2:20; Romans 8:37).

"Our growth in grace, our joy, our usefulness,—all depend upon our union with Christ. It is by communion with Him, daily, hourly,—by abiding in Him,—that we are to grow in grace. . . .

"Consecrate yourself to God in the morning; make this your very first work."[22]

What the Bible Teaches About

JUDGMENT FOR ALL OF HUMANITY

10

THE JUDGMENT

1. What will God judge? Ecclesiastes 12:14

   ____

2. How many will appear before the judgment? 2 Corinthians 5:10

   ____

THE JUDGMENT IN ACTION

3. Who is the judge? John 5:22

   ____

4. Where are our actions recorded? Revelation 20:12

   ____

5. Who are the witnesses? Matthew 18:10

   ____

6. Who is the attorney? 1 John 2:1

   ____

7. By what code will we be judged? James 2:12

   ____

8. What will be the sentence? Matthew 25:31–46

   ____

WHAT MUST I DO?

1. Believe and obey Jesus (John 5:24).
2. Love God and keep the commandments (Ecclesiastes 12:13).

I accept Jesus as my attorney. I desire to be faithful to God and to respect all His commandments.

____

SIGNATURE

ADDITIONAL STUDY

There will be a judgment. God has established a day to judge (Acts 17:31). Even hidden things will be judged (Romans 2:16).

Everyone will appear before the judge. We shall all stand before the judgment seat of Christ (Romans 14:10). Even the evil angels will be judged (Jude 6). Everyone will have to answer for their actions (Matthew 12:36; Romans 14:12; Ecclesiastes 11:9). The judgment will begin at the house of God (1 Peter 4:17). The just and the wicked will be judged (Ecclesiastes 3:17). It is impossible to deceive God (Galatians 6:7).

The records. The judgment is carried out with the help of the records that are in heaven. (Revelation 20:12). There are several books:

1. The book of life (Revelation 20:12).
2. The book of remembrance (Malachi 3:16).
3. The book of sins (Isaiah 65:6, 7; Matthew 12:36, 37).

The standard of judgment. The supreme standard is God's holy law (Romans 7:7; James 2:12; Ecclesiastes 12:13, 14). We will also be judged according to the teachings and the gospel of Jesus (John 12:48; Romans 2:16).

The reality of the judgment

The prophet Daniel saw the dramatic moment of the beginning of the judgment (Daniel 7:9, 10).

Diverse religious authorities refer to that moment. "Before the judgment seat of God each man must render an account of his own life, whether he has done good or evil."[23]

"Jesus will return to the world at the end of time, to exercise his power as sovereign judge. That judgment called public, universal, ultimate, is necessary to justify divine providence, glorify Jesus Christ, gladden the just and confuse the wicked."[24]

The time of the judgment

Daniel, in his prophecy in chapter 8 verse 14, establishes that at the end of the period of 2,300 years, "the sanctuary [would] be cleansed."

The sanctuary was the Jewish center of worship. Once a year, a very important judgment ceremony would take place. The Bible explains that the true sanctuary is in heaven (Hebrews 8:2, 5). The purification of this heavenly sanctuary is the beginning of the investigative judgment, which began at the end of the 2,300 years, in other words, in 1844.

The defense attorney

Jesus plays an important role in the judgment. The Father assigned Him the specific task of judging (John 5:22, 27; Acts 10:42). "God, in order to glorify the humanity of his divine son, entrusted to him the judgment of men. We must all stand before the judgment seat of Christ."[25]

Jesus' most important task is that of Attorney and Intercessor. Daniel says that with the judgment in action, Christ presents Himself and is taken to the Father (Daniel 7:9, 13). There, He intercedes for us (1 Timothy 2:5; Hebrews 7:25). The sinner must come to Jesus with confidence (Hebrews 4:16). When we have sincerely repented, after confessing all our sins, Jesus takes care of our cause and acts as our effective attorney (1 John 1:9; 2:1).

Assurance in the judgment

The assurance for the judgment consists in separating completely from sin (Ezekiel 18:20–22, 27). Then Jesus will come and reward every person according to their works (Matthew 16:27). There will be no problem for all who have stayed firm and faithful until the end (Revelation 2:10; 3:5). By believing in Jesus, walking in His light, and trusting fully in Him, we can have absolute certainty of having a favorable outcome at the judgment (1 John 1:7; John 5:24).

What the Bible Teaches About

THE TEN COMMANDMENTS

11

THE IMPORTANCE OF THE TEN COMMANDMENTS

1. Who wrote them and how? Exodus 31:18

2. What other name do the Ten Commandments have, and what do they reveal? 1 John 3:4

3. To whom does the law take us? Galatians 3:24

4. Review the Ten Commandments. Exodus 20:3–17

VALIDITY OF THE HOLY LAW

5. What was Jesus' attitude toward the law? John 15:10

6. Did Jesus make any changes to the commandments? Matthew 5:17, 18

7. Can anyone change the Ten Commandments? Ecclesiastes 3:14

WHAT MUST I DO?

1. Love God and keep His law (John 14:15).
2. Keep the commandments (Psalm 119:44).
3. Respect all the commandments (James 2:10).

I accept God's holy law. I will strive, with God's help, to respect the Ten Commandments.

SIGNATURE

ADDITIONAL STUDY

The importance of the law. God's law is the standard of truth (Isaiah 8:20) and the copy of God's character. Both are *holy* (1 Peter 1:6; Romans 7:12); *righteous* (John 17:25; Psalm 119:172); *perfect* (Matthew 5:48; Psalm 19:7, 8); *eternal* (Hebrews 13:8; Psalm 111:7, 8).

Validity of God's law. God is eternal (Malachi 3:6). His law is also eternal (Psalm 119:152). Christ did not change the law; He confirmed it (Matthew 5:17, 18; Isaiah 42:21). Jesus' mother, as well as His disciples, apostles, and followers, respected the holy law (Luke 23:56; Romans 7:22; 2 Peter 2:21; James 1:25; 1 John 2:3, 7).

Christians must keep the holy law. The law is of great usefulness for the Christian (Romans 2:18; Psalm 119:104, 165). The true demonstration of God's love is to keep His commandments (John 14:15, 21; 15:10). The redeemed will keep the holy law (Romans 2:13; Revelation 14:12; 1 John 2:3–6). God helps us to respect the holy law (Hebrews 10:16; John 15:5; Romans 8:3, 4).

Blessings we receive when we keep the commandments

The universe, God's creation, is ruled by natural laws. All moral, social, commercial, and international order is governed by laws. Likewise, God instituted moral and spiritual laws. These are like the wise rules of a father for the upright formation of his children. The biblical teaching is clear about the need to respect the holy commandments. "Not every one that saith unto me, Lord, Lord, shall enter into the kingdom of heaven; but he that doeth the will of my father which is in heaven" (Matthew 7:21). Since God will bring all works to judgment, we must all keep the commandments (Ecclesiastes 12:13). Blessings are promised to those who keep the law: They will have peace (Isaiah 48:18; Psalm 119:165); Jehovah shall exalt them (Deuteronomy 28:1).

The law and grace

Nobody is saved by keeping the law, but rather by the redemptive grace of Jesus (Galatians 2:16). However, the law has an important and necessary part in salvation: it indicates to us what sin is (1 John 3:4). Like a mirror, it shows us our desperate condition (James 1:23–25). Then it takes us to Christ who saves us (Romans 10:4; Galatians 3:24). When, with God's help, we are saved, we will respect the holy law because grace does not invalidate God's law (Romans 3:31).

God's law was not abolished

Jesus taught with clarity that God's holy law does not change (Matthew 5:17, 18). Therefore, in order not to be confused, it is good to differentiate between God's moral law that is eternal and the ceremonial laws that represented Christ and His sacrifice, and that, therefore, ended with His death on the cross (Colossians 2:14; Ephesians 2:15).

Moral versus ceremonial laws

Moral law: spiritual (Romans 7:14); royal (James 2:8); given by God (Deuteronomy 4:12, 13); written in stone (Exodus 31:18); unchanging (Psalm 111:7, 8); not abolished (Romans 3:31).

Ceremonial law: carnal (Hebrews 7:16); ritual (Colossians 2:14); given by Moses (Leviticus 1:1–3); written in a book (Deuteronomy 31:24); temporal (Hebrews 10:1); was abolished (Colossians 2:14).

God's Ten Commandments

The Ten Commandments are recorded in Exodus 20:3–17. Nobody has the right to change these commandments; neither should anybody add nor remove anything (Ecclesiastes 3:14; Revelation 22:18, 19). Jesus never authorized anyone to make any change; on the contrary, He energetically rebuked whoever tried to exchange the law for human tradition (Matthew 15:3, 6, 9).

What the Bible Teaches About

THE BEST DAY TO REST

12

THE DAY OF REST GIVEN BY GOD

1. According to God's law, which day is the day of rest? Exodus 20:8–11

____

2. Whom does the Sabbath benefit? Mark 2:27

____

THE HISTORY OF THE SEVENTH DAY: THE SABBATH

3. Who instituted the Sabbath and when did He do so? Genesis 2:1–3

____

4. On what day did our Lord Jesus Christ rest? Luke 4:16

____

5. What day did Jesus' mother, Mary, keep? Luke 23:56

____

6. What day did Jesus' apostles keep? Acts 17:2

____

7. What day will be kept in heaven? Isaiah 66:22, 23

____

WHAT MUST I DO?

1. Be careful not to desecrate the Sabbath (Isaiah 56:2).
2. Honor the Sabbath, doing God's will (Isaiah 58:13, 14).
3. Obey God rather than men (Acts 5:29).

I believe that the Sabbath is the day of the Lord. I desire to be faithful to God and observe it correctly.

____

SIGNATURE

ADDITIONAL STUDY

Venerable history of the Sabbath. The Sabbath was given at creation (Genesis 2:1–3). Abraham respected it (Genesis 26:5). It was sanctified by the Hebrews before the written law was given (Exodus 16:21–30) and established in the holy law (Exodus 20:8–11). It was kept by Jesus (Luke 6:5; 4:16; Mark 1:21), respected by Mary (Luke 23:56), and kept by the apostles (Acts 13:14, 44; 17:2; 18:4). It will be respected in heaven (Isaiah 66:22, 23).

No one has the right to change it. God is unchangeable (Malachi 3:6). Jesus is unchanging (Hebrews 13:8). Neither men nor institutions have the right to change the law of God (Matthew 5:18, 19; 15:6, 9; Ecclesiastes 3:14).

The Christian must follow the example of Jesus. Jesus respected the commandments and kept the holy Sabbath (Luke 4:16). The true Christian follows Jesus' example in all things (1 Peter 2:21; 1 John 2:6; 3:3; John 14:15).

The Lord's Day

The phrase "Lord's day" refers to the Sabbath (Revelation 1:10; Matthew 12:8). The Sabbath is a perpetual reminder of God's creative power. Through the centuries, the Sabbath has been the seventh day of the week. The Bible identifies it as the seventh day in several texts (Exodus 16:26; 20:8–11; 35:2; Leviticus 23:3; Ezekiel 46:1; Luke 13:14). "Sabbath, in the Hebrew language, signifies rest, and is the seventh day of the week."[26]

Sunday is not the day of rest

In the New Testament, the expression "first day of the week" appears eight times, referring to Sunday (Matthew 28:1; Mark 16:2, 9; Luke 24:1; John 20:1, 19; Acts 20:7; 1 Corinthians 16:2). Every time we see "first day of the week," the day or event is not given any religious significance. On the other hand, the Sabbath is referred to fifty-nine times by the word *sábbaton*, which means "rest." "You may read the Bible from Genesis to Revelation, and you will not find a single line authorizing the sanctification of Sunday. The Scriptures enforce the religious observance of Saturday, a day which we never sanctify."[27]

How was the change made?

The Bible predicts serious attacks against God's law (Daniel 7:25; 8:12). Likewise, the apostles warn Christians about the apostasy and the introduction of heresies into the bosom of the church (Acts 20:28, 30; 2 Thessalonians 2:3, 4; Romans 1:25).

The change was not made by Christ or the apostles; rather, it came on little by little in a church that had separated itself from the eternal principles of God's law. Thousands of pagans who were not fully converted and who worshiped the sun came into the church. The worship of the sun was on the first day of the week. For some time, both days were observed, until Constantine issued his famous decree ordering to sanctify only Sunday.

Constantine's decree states: "All judges and the people in the city should rest, and the work in all crafts should cease, on holy Sunday."[28]

Dr. Augustus Neander, a renowned church history professor from Berlin, states: "The festival of Sunday, like all other festivals, was always only a human ordinance, and it was far from the intentions of the apostles to establish a Divine command in this respect, far from them, and from the early apostolic Church, to transfer the laws of the Sabbath to Sunday."[29] God could never approve of these changes. Our Lord Jesus severely rebuked anyone who placed human teachings above divine ones (Psalm 89:33, 34; Matthew 15:3, 9).

The seal of God

God has tests of obedience to determine who His faithful children are. In Eden, it was the tree of the knowledge of good and evil. Now, the Lord has a seal by which He knows who are His own (2 Timothy 2:19). With this seal He will indicate or seal His children (Revelation 7:2, 3). Because of this, keeping the Sabbath is a sign between God and His children (Ezekiel 20:12, 20).

What the Bible Teaches About

THE OBSERVANCE OF THE SABBATH

13

THE CORRECT WAY TO RESPECT THE SABBATH

1. What did God do with the Sabbath? Genesis 2:1–3

____

2. On what day should preparations be made? Exodus 16:22, 23

____

3. When does the Sabbath begin? Leviticus 23:32

____

4. What must we abstain from on the Sabbath? Exodus 20:10

____

5. Where must we attend on the Sabbath? Luke 4:16

____

6. What can be done on the Sabbath? Matthew 12:12

____

BLESSINGS FOR THOSE WHO OBEY GOD

7. What is God's promise for those who are faithful? Psalm 37:25

____

8. What protection will God give to those who obey Him? Deuteronomy 11:13–15

____

WHAT MUST I DO?

1. Faithfully obey what God commands (James 4:17).
2. Trust fully in Jesus (Philippians 4:13).

I will be obedient to God and to keep faithfully the holy Sabbath, following Jesus' example.

____

SIGNATURE

ADDITIONAL STUDY

The way to respect the Sabbath. God requires that we cease doing regular work (Exodus 20:8–11; 31:13–18; 34:21). We must not buy or sell (Nehemiah 10:31; 13:15–20). The most appropriate thing is to attend a religious worship service (Leviticus 26:2; Hebrews 10:25; Luke 4:16; Acts 17:2). It is also good to do good works and serve others (Mark 3:4; Matthew 12:12).

God helps those who obey Him. It is necessary to do God's will (Matthew 7:21). We must obey everything God commands (James 2:10). The reason for obedience is love (John 14:15). When we keep the Sabbath, we receive the promised blessings (Deuteronomy 11:26, 27; Isaiah 41:10; Psalm 37:25; Isaiah 58:13, 14).

The restoration of the Sabbath

Due to the apostasy of the Christian church, Constantine designated the "holy Sunday" as the Roman day of rest rather than the Sabbath. The Bible had predicted that the observance of the holy commandment would be restored by a people called to repair the breaches (Isaiah 58:12, 13). These people "keep the commandments of God" (Revelation 12:17; Isaiah 66:23). That is why the Seventh-day Adventist Church respects the Lord's day. Each Sabbath, in every corner of the world, millions of people gather to praise and worship God.

Sabbath worship

The Sabbath celebration generally takes place in the morning and includes a Bible study and a worship service, including a sermon presented by a minister or layperson. The faithful participate actively through song, prayer, Bible readings, and offerings. Often, the afternoon is dedicated to rest, reading, meditation, missionary outreach, or a meeting for the youth.

What is the truth?

Since so many millions of Christians observe Sunday as a holy day, many ask themselves: "Who is right?" It's very easy to resolve. We must ask ourselves with absolute sincerity, "What is the truth?" Then, when we have discovered it in the Bible, we have to obey it faithfully.

We know that the Bible contains the truth (John 17:17). The Bible establishes the Sabbath as the only day of rest. And God's word endures forever (Isaiah 40:8).

Jesus is the purest revelation of the truth. His mission was to "bear witness unto the truth" (John 18:37). Jesus kept the Sabbath from sundown Friday to sundown Saturday per the Bible guidelines. He taught us that we are to follow His example in everything (John 13:15). "Jesus Christ the same yesterday, and to day, and for ever." (Hebrews 13:8).

The law of God is the truth (Psalm 119:142). The law specifies clearly the sacredness of the Sabbath, and the commandments have been established forever (Psalm 119:152). God is the supreme source of truth; Jesus, the Bible, and the law are exponents of the truth, and they each teach the sacredness of the Sabbath. What shall we do? Hopefully, we will say: "I have chosen the way of truth" (Psalm 119:30).

Why do I keep the Sabbath?

If someone were to ask, "Why do you respect the Sabbath?" we could give six indisputable reasons: (1) I believe that there is one Lord's day, the Sabbath (Mark 2:27, 28). (2) I want to be an upright Christian. That is why I have to follow in Jesus' footsteps (1 Peter 2:21). Jesus zealously respected the Sabbath, and He said that He did not come to change the commandments (Matthew 5:17, 18). Therefore, I must respect it. (3) There is no doubt that if Christ, His mother, and the apostles were on the earth today, they would faithfully keep the Sabbath (Hebrews 13:8). (4) I want to be a faithful child of God; He created the Sabbath. (5) I believe in the Bible. It tells me explicitly that the Sabbath is holy. (6) I want to be with Jesus in heaven. The Sabbath will be kept there (Isaiah 66:22, 23).

What the Bible Teaches About

CHARACTERISTICS OF THE TRUE CHURCH

14

FOUNDATION AND BASIS

1. Who founded the Christian church? Matthew 16:16–18

   ____

2. Who is the foundation of the church? Ephesians 2:20

   ____

THE ORGANIZATION OF THE CHURCH

3. Who are the leaders of the church? Ephesians 4:11, 12

   ____

4. What is the triple mission of the church? Matthew 4:23

   ____

5. How should the church be governed? Acts 6:1–4

   ____

THE CHARACTERISTICS OF THE TRUE CHURCH

6. What example should the church follow? John 13:15

   ____

7. What is the standard of conduct for the church? Revelation 12:17

   ____

8. What gift will the church possess? Revelation 19:10

   ____

WHAT MUST I DO?

1. Join the true church (Acts 2:41).
2. Stay faithful and firm (2 Peter 1:10–12).

I believe that Jesus founded the church. I desire to join it and to be faithful to the end.

____

SIGNATURE

ADDITIONAL STUDY

Christ, the foundation. Christ is the true foundation of the church (Ephesians 2:20). Nobody can put down a different foundation (1 Corinthians 3:11).

The church and its leaders. Christ is the head of the church (Ephesians 1:22). List of authorities (Ephesians 4:11, 12). Qualifications of ministers (1 Timothy 3:1–7; Titus 1:7–9). Deacons and their qualifications (1 Timothy 3:8–13). The deaconesses (1 Timothy 3:11). Members call each other brothers and sisters (Matthew 23:8, 9).

Rites of the church:

1. Baptism by immersion (Matthew 3:13–17).
2. Lord's Supper, or Communion (1 Corinthians 11:23–29).
3. Foot washing (John 13:4–17).
4. Placing of hands to ordain ministers or deacons (Acts 6:1–6).
5. Anointing of the sick (James 5:14, 15).
6. Holy matrimony (Matthew 19:4–6).

The mission of the church. The church is to be a pillar and bastion of the truth (1 Timothy 3:15), pure and holy (Ephesians 5:27), and to preach the gospel (Matthew 24:14).

The Christian church

The church was founded by Jesus. The word *church* comes from the Greek *ekklesía*, and it means "assembly" or "congregation." It is a group of human beings who believe and obey Jesus and His doctrine.

The great drama of the church

During the first century, the church stayed faithful to Jesus' genuine doctrine. However, heresies and serious errors started to come in, which the apostles had rebuked (Romans 1:18–32; 2 Peter 2:1, 2; Titus 1:14; Colossians 2:8). The errors included core doctrines. They also altered the church's form of government so much so that "it cast down the truth to the ground" (Daniel 8:12). This unfortunate situation would last 1,260 years (Daniel 7:25; Revelation 12:6, 14; 13:5), from A.D. 538 until 1798.

The restoration of the truth

After that long period of spiritual darkness, the truth would revive gloriously to be preached in the form of a three-part message (Revelation 14:6–12).

Characteristics of the true church

The true church must possess the faith of Jesus (Revelation 14:12). It will respect the commandments of the law of God (Revelation 14:12). It will have the visible manifestation of the Spirit of prophecy (Revelation 19:10). It will respect the holy Sabbath of the Lord (Exodus 20:8–11). It will be guided in everything by what God's holy Word says (2 Timothy 3:16). It will have a dynamic, three-pronged evangelistic program (Matthew 4:23). It will announce the imminent judgment (Revelation 14:7). It will preach with power about the second coming of Jesus (Titus 2:13).

Seventh-day Adventist Church

The Adventist Church emerged at the time indicated by prophecy and as a result of a deep study of the Holy Bible. The true church has four distinctive characteristics: (1) *unity* of doctrine, rites, and regulations (Ephesians 4:3–6), (2) *holiness* in the life and conduct of the members (1 Thessalonians 4:2–7), (3) *universality* (Matthew 24:14), (4) *apostolicity* (Jude 3).

The Adventist Church develops its mission in the three phases that our Lord Jesus Christ commanded. Thousands of ministers preach the gospel in person, on the radio, on television, and in publications produced by more than seventy-five publishing houses. The church has 8,500 schools, colleges, and universities. In the health field, the church maintains 168 hospitals, 138 nursing homes and retirement centers, 442 clinics, and 34 orphanages. The authorities of the church are those indicated in the holy Bible. The church is governed by representatives of its members, just as it was in the time of the apostles. Likewise, the church is set up and runs per the guidelines of Jesus Christ and the apostles. The church has restored the eternal truths of the gospel. The holy Bible, the teachings of our Lord Jesus Christ, the apostles, and the law of God are the standards of conduct of the church and the believers. The Adventist Church is the historic continuation of the permanent people that God has had as proclaimers of the truth. It maintains that Christian doctrines must be practiced in every aspect of life.

What the Bible Teaches About

THE DISCIPLESHIP OF THE FOLLOWERS OF JESUS CHRIST

THE MISSION OF THE CHURCH

1. What is the mission of God's children? Matthew 28:19

   ____

2. What missionary goal has God given us? Matthew 24:14

   ____

3. How does God consider us when carrying out the mission? 2 Corinthians 5:20

   ____

THE METHODS WE ARE TO FOLLOW

4. What are two qualities a disciple must have? Matthew 10:16

   ____

5. What are the two phases that the mission must have? Acts 20:20; 5:42

   ____

6. How does God want us to carry out this work? Luke 10:1

   ____

THE SOURCE OF SUCCESS IN THE MISSION

7. What promise did Jesus give us? Matthew 28:20

   ____

8. What is the secret of power? Acts 1:8

   ____

9. Who guarantees the result? 1 Corinthians 3:6–7

   ____

WHAT MUST I DO?

1. Accept the invitation that God extends to me (Matthew 4:19).
2. Keep a joyful attitude to carry out this work (Isaiah 52:7).
3. Abide in Jesus every day in order to have the desire to testify (John 15:27).

I desire to become a part of the mission by being a disciple of Jesus Christ, preaching the gospel, and winning people for His kingdom.

____

SIGNATURE

ADDITIONAL STUDY

The call to service

Every follower of Jesus Christ is called specifically for a mission (1 Peter 2:9). The mission is worldwide, and it will continue until Christ returns (Matthew 24:14). It is the same mission that the father entrusted to Christ (John 17:18, 20:21), and it must be carried out in a public and private way (Acts 20:20, 5:42).

Whoever participates in this ministry brings joy to heaven (Luke 15:7, 10). It produces satisfaction and joy for the disciple (1 Thessalonians 2:19, 20; Psalm 126:5, 6). It was the same joy that allowed Christ to endure the cross (Hebrews 12:2).

God gives us gifts for ministry (Ephesians 4:8, 11–13, 17). In this work each one has a designated place (Mark 13:34). We are sent with the power of Christ, in His name, and we will have His company (Matthew 28:18–20). For the apostle Paul, this was a "necessity" (1 Corinthians 9:16). Whoever fulfills this ministry has a reward (Daniel 12:3).

The New Testament and history

The passion to save others, the fruit of the presence of the Holy Spirit, was evident in both the primitive church and the post-apostolic one. The desire to be a disciple of Jesus Christ has characterized all true believers throughout history.

For those in the early church, preaching the gospel was not just one more option within the value scale of the Christian life; rather, it was the main purpose of life. It was the essence, the basis, the foundation, and the backbone of believing and trusting in God.

Passion for discipleship

This passion is what led George Whitfield, the famous British evangelist, to say, "Oh, Lord, give me souls or take mine," and missionary Henry Martin to say in India, "Here I will burn for God."

Dwight Moody expressed similar sentiments: "My Savior, use me for whatever purpose and in whatever way you need me." John Mackenzie prayed on his knees on the banks of the Lottie River: "Oh, Lord, send me to the darkest place on earth."

John Hunt, a missionary in the Fiji islands, prayed while he was dying, "Lord, save Fiji: save these people; oh Lord, have mercy on Fiji."

David Brainerd, a well-known missionary, said while working among the Delaware Indians, "I don't care where I live or what hardships I go through, as long as I win souls for Christ. While I sleep, I dream about this. As soon as I wake up, the first thing I think about is this great work."

The greatest work

The prolific Christian author Ellen G. White, in the May 4, 1893, issue of *The Youth's Instructor*, expressed this:

"The work above all work,—the business above all others which should draw and engage the energies of the soul,—is the work of saving souls for whom Christ has died. Make this the main, the important work of your life. Make it your special life-work."[30]

The best profession of all

It was the passion for the discipleship that burned in Spurgeon's heart that led him to prepare a series of lecture topics titled "What Is Soul Winning?" for students at the theological seminary who were studying for what he called "the greatest of all professions: winning souls."

In it he said: "Soul winning is the main occupation of the Christian minister; and it certainly should be for every true believer. Each one of us should say like Simon Peter: 'I will go fishing,' and work like Paul 'that some may be saved.' "

What the Bible Teaches About

THE HAPPY OCCASION OF BAPTISM

16

TRUE BAPTISM

1. Why must we get baptized? Matthew 28:18–20

____

2. What is the correct way to baptize? Matthew 3:13–16

____

3. Is baptism required to be saved? Mark 16:16

____

4. What does baptism symbolize? Romans 6:3

____

5. What statement did God make at Jesus' baptism? Matthew 3:17

____

THE WONDERFUL RESULTS OF BAPTISM

6. What two blessings are received with baptism? Acts 2:38

____

7. What divine institution do the baptized join? Acts 2:41, 42, 47

____

8. What glorious experience does the baptized individual obtain? Romans 6:4

____

WHAT MUST I DO?

1. Believe in the Lord Jesus (Acts 8:37).
2. Abandon sin (Romans 6:11–13).
3. Ask for baptism (Acts 8:35–38).
4. Respond to God's calling without delay (Hebrews 3:15).

I believe in baptism by immersion. I wish to be baptized as Jesus was.

____

SIGNATURE

ADDITIONAL STUDY

What is baptism?

The word *baptism* comes from a Greek word meaning "to sink" or "to submerge." Baptism is a symbol of death to a life of unbelief and birth to a new experience in Christ. It is a reminder of the death and resurrection of our Lord Jesus Christ (Romans 6:3, 4). Our Lord Jesus Christ, even though He did not need to be baptized, did so as an example for us (John 13:15). Jesus indicated that we should be baptized in name of the holy Godhead (Matthew 28:19).

Who can be baptized?

All who meet the required conditions may be baptized. Conditions include believing in the Lord Jesus (Acts 8:36–38), repenting of all sin (Acts 2:38), confessing all sin (Proverbs 28:13), knowing doctrine (Matthew 28:20), practicing doctrine (Matthew 7:21), and asking for baptism (Acts 8:36).

When we apply these conditions, it is clear that a very young child cannot be baptized, but a minor who understands doctrine can be. If we have been baptized without our consent, without a complete comprehension of all truth, or in an incorrect way, or if we have strayed from the truth, the Bible authorizes a new baptism (Acts 19:1–5).

Forms of baptism

As the definition of *baptism* indicates, and according to Jesus' and the apostles' examples, baptism must be by immersion. In other words, the person should be covered completely with water. Jesus "went up straightway out of the water" (Matthew 3:16). John baptized where "there was much water" (John 3:23). "They went down both into the water" (Acts 8:38). There is only one true baptism (Ephesians 4:5).

Cardinal James Gibbons says: "For several centuries after the establishing of Christianity, Baptism was *usually* conferred by immersion, but since the twelfth century, the practice of baptising by infusion has prevailed in the Catholic church."[31]

Monsignor John Straubinger, commenting on a verse about baptism, says, "It refers to the baptism of the early Christians, which were baptized by completely submerging in water. Just as Christ was buried upon His death, we are buried in the waters of baptism."[32]

The result of baptism

When this ritual is done sincerely, it is a public testimony of turning away from the sinful past life and beginning a new life in Christ. The forgiveness of past sins is promised in addition to an abundant measure of the Holy Spirit (Acts 2:38). Also, the baptized individual has a new relationship with Christ (Galatians 3:27). He becomes a member of Christ's church (Acts 2:41).

After baptism

The old life has been buried in the liquid tomb. Now a new life begins (Romans 6:4). Henceforth, the way of living must change completely (Ephesians 4:22–24). Normally, there should be no more sin (1 John 3:9). Now, we have to be careful with evil and trust in God, and the evil one will not touch us (1 John 5:18). Then, the great work of sanctification begins (Romans 6:22); this consists of a constant perfecting of our character. This task lasts the whole life. There must not be standstills or relapses (Proverbs 4:18).

The key to sanctification is a perfect union with our Lord Jesus (John 15:4, 5). Without Him, we can do nothing. With Him, everything is possible (Philippians 4:13). There will be a constant struggle with the "old man," whom we should "crucify" to allow space for Christ to live in us (Galatians 2:20). We must never lose heart, but rather persevere until the end (Matthew 24:13).

What the Bible Teaches About

THE CHRISTIAN LIFESTYLE

17

NEW LIFE

1. What change happens when I accept Jesus? 2 Corinthians 5:17

____

2. What wonderful experience will we have? 1 Thessalonians 5:23

____

3. What is the correct attitude when facing trials? 1 Peter 4:12, 13

____

DEVOTIONAL LIFE

4. What is the indispensable daily spiritual food? Deuteronomy 17:19

____

5. How do we establish communion with God? 1 Peter 4:7

____

A LIFE OF WORSHIP

6. What day is dedicated to worshiping God? Isaiah 58:12–14

____

7. What is the ideal place for worshiping God? Luke 4:16

____

A LIFE OF CHRISTIAN WITNESS

8. What mission did God entrust to us? Matthew 24:14; 28:19

____

9. What essential preparation must we have? 1 Peter 3:15

____

SPIRITUAL GUIDES

10. Who are our human guides? 1 Thessalonians 5:12, 13

____

11. Who is our supreme guide? Colossians 2:6, 7

____

I believe in God's help and in following Jesus, and I will strive to live as an upright Christian.

____

SIGNATURE

ADDITIONAL STUDY

A holy life

By surrendering ourselves to the Lord and joining His church, we begin a new life. Our conduct, character, and ideals have changes. Before, our first interest was in material things; now, we live the way Jesus shows us: "Seek ye first the kingdom of God, and his righteousness; and all these things shall be added unto you" (Matthew 6:33). We have before us the lofty goal of being holy (1 Peter 1:15, 16) because that is the will of God for our lives (1 Thessalonians 4:3–5).

Life at home

The new life can be seen at home. The relationship between spouses will be guided by respect, understanding, and love (Ephesians 5:22–29). The education of the children will be of primary interest; the parents will be firm and wise (Ephesians 6:4). The children will respond by obeying gladly (Ephesians 6:1).

Social life

We live the Christian life not only in the church but in every place and at every moment. It is an emotional adventure to live like Christ. The Bible recommends that we are to be hard workers (2 Thessalonians 3:10–12). As far as our relationship with everyone else, Christ established the precious golden rule: Whatever we wish to have done to us, we must do for others (Matthew 7:12). Be very careful with the tongue and with words (Matthew 5:37; Colossians 4:6). Authorities deserve our respect and obedience, so long as their words do not conflict with Scripture (1 Peter 2:13, 14; Romans 13:1–3), without forgetting that God is above all (Acts 5:29).

Spiritual life

The spiritual life is private and public; publicly it is developed through church activities that have been planned to benefit, nourish, encourage, and perfect the faithful.

- **Worship services.**
    a. Sabbath School takes place every Sabbath morning and consists of the systematic study of the Bible. Every member studies the lesson at home daily.
    b. Worship service consists of songs, reading the Bible, and the preaching of a spiritual topic. It is the main service that all members and friends attend.
    c. AYS/Pathfinders usually takes place on Sabbath afternoon and is a special meeting for young people and children.
    d. Prayer meeting generally takes place on Wednesday nights and is dedicated to Bible study, prayer, and fellowship.

- **Authorities of the church.** The pastor or head elder is in charge of the spiritual care of the members. The pastor is named by the conference. All church matters are decided by the church board.
- **Offerings.** The church is supported by the members, who voluntarily give tithes and offerings, which belong to God and are used to support the various activities of the church in the world as well as locally. One of the great privileges of being a Christian is to give generously for God's work.
- **Missionary work.** Every member of the church is called to cooperate in the sacred task of sharing the message of salvation with others. One of the deepest joys in life is taking others to the feet of Jesus.
- **The universal church.** The Adventist church exists throughout the world. It is organized perfectly to fulfill the commission given by Jesus to preach the gospel.
- **The members.** The members of the church sometimes call one another brother or sister (Matthew 23:8). United by the same faith and the same hope, they help and love one another with brotherly love (1 Peter 1:22).

The triumph of the church

The church that works now will achieve a glorious triumph when Christ comes for the second time. The church will not be free of problems, anguish, dangers, and cruel persecution, but the Lord will take care of it and preserve it until the end (Matthew 28:20). Those who stay faithful to God and His church will triumph with her.

What the Bible Teaches About

HEALTH PRINCIPLES AND GUIDELINES FOR LIVING

18

THE BODY IS GOD'S TEMPLE

1. How does God consider the human body? 1 Corinthians 6:19, 20

   ____

2. In what two aspects is God interested? 3 John 2

   ____

HEALTH PRINCIPLES

3. What is the basic principle for eating? 1 Corinthians 10:31

   ____

4. What meats are not acceptable? Leviticus 11:3–20

   ____

5. Why do we stay away from alcoholic beverages? Proverbs 20:1

   ____

6. Why is it best not to use tobacco, coffee, and stimulating drugs? 1 Corinthians 3:16, 17

   ____

STANDARDS OF LIVING

7. What should personal appearance be like? 1 Timothy 2:9, 10

   ____

8. Why do we not attend inappropriate shows? 1 Peter 2:21

   ____

WHAT MUST I DO?

1. Strive to live a perfect Christian life (Matthew 5:48).
2. Follow Jesus' example in all things (1 John 2:6).

I believe that my body is the temple of the Holy Spirit. I will abstain from all harmful foods or beverages.

____

SIGNATURE

ADDITIONAL STUDY

A pure and spotless church. We are a chosen people (1 Peter 2:9). The Christian is *in* the world but is not *of* the world (1 John 2:15–17; James 4:4). The church must be holy and spotless (Ephesians 5:25–27). It must be an example for the world (Matthew 5:16). We must abstain from all evil (1 Corinthians 9:25–27).

Dynamic Christianity. The Christian has integrity (Psalm 15:1–5). He is honest in his business transactions (Proverbs 20:10). His thoughts are elevated (Philippians 4:8). The Christian is careful with words (Ephesians 4:25–29). The Christian avoids the fruits of the flesh and practices the ones of the spirit (Galatians 5:19–26).

Christian modesty. Christian modesty is recommended (1 Timothy 2:9, 10). Dispense with superfluous external adornment (Isaiah 3:18–23; Genesis 35:1–4; Jeremiah 4:30). True beauty emanates from a life consecrated to God (Proverbs 31:30).

The Christian and health

When worshiping God, we do it with our spirit and our body; therefore, both must be irreproachable (1 Thessalonians 5:23). God considers our body to be a temple (1 Corinthians 6:19). Any attack against the health of the body is a grave sin before God (1 Corinthians 3:16, 17). "Our bodies must be kept in the best possible condition physically, and under the most spiritual influences.

". . . Those who thus shorten their lives by disregarding nature's laws are guilty of robbery toward God."[33]

Temperance is an important principle in the life of the Christian (Luke 21:34).

The use of meat

God did not plan for people to eat meat. The diet given by the Lord was plant-based (Genesis 1:29). After the flood, the survivors received provisional permission to consume meat (Genesis 9:3). Because man became accustomed to the carnivorous diet, God indicated specifically which meats were acceptable. These indications are found in the book of Leviticus, chapter 11. In general, the instructions are the following:

- Meat. The meat of animals with a split hoof and that also chew their cud can be eaten. If one or both of these characteristics are lacking, the meat is not acceptable.
- Fish. The ones with both fins and scales may be eaten.
- Birds. Birds of prey or nocturnal birds are not acceptable for food.
- Blood. The Bible strictly forbids the use of blood as food. (Leviticus 17:13, 14).

Alcohol and tobacco

The Bible recommends abstaining from all alcoholic beverages (Proverbs 23:20; 20:1; Isaiah 28:7; Luke 1:15; 1 Corinthians 6:10; Ephesians 5:18).

Tobacco was not known in Bible times. However, its use has spread through the entire world. Men, women, and children fall victims to this vice. Every cigarette contains approximately thirty-five poisons. Medical science warns us of the terrible effects of tobacco. It affects the lungs, the sense of smell, the stomach, vision, and the arteries that feed the heart. The relationship between smoking and cancer has been proven. Whoever desires to be a child of God must leave behind this terrible vice (2 Timothy 2:21). It is also best to avoid coffee, tea, and other stimulant drugs and poisons.

Jesus, our example, our strength

The Christian life is a constant struggle. The secret of triumph consists in following in Jesus' footsteps (1 Peter 2:21). It requires a spirit of sacrifice (Luke 9:23; 1 Corinthians 9:26, 27) and abandoning wrong customs (Titus 2:12, 13). A reform of habits is necessary (Romans 12:2).

What the Bible Teaches About

WHAT HAPPENS WHEN A PERSON DIES

19

LIFE

1. Who created man, and how did He do it? Genesis 1:27; 2:7

____

DEATH

2. Why do we have to die? Romans 6:23; 5:12

____

3. What is death? Ecclesiastes 12:7

____

4. To what does Jesus compare death? John 11:11–13

____

5. Does the person who died know anything? Ecclesiastes 9:5, 6

____

6. What happens with the soul? Ezekiel 18:4

____

7. Should we consult the dead? Deuteronomy 18:10, 11

____

WHAT MUST I DO?

1. Take comfort in the hope of the resurrection (1 Thessalonians 4:13–18).
2. Believe in Jesus (John 11:25).
3. Remain in Jesus and in the truth until the day in which God makes us immortal (Romans 2:7).

I trust in God's promises. I surrender my life to Jesus in order to have eternal life.

____

SIGNATURE

ADDITIONAL STUDY

Death is the cessation of life. Death is a return to dust (Ecclesiastes 3:20). No more suffering or rejoicing (Ecclesiastes 9:5, 6). The dead cease to be (Psalm 104:29). Thoughts come to an end (Psalm 146:4). No more participation in the concerns of the living (Job 14:21; Psalm 6:5).

Immortality. Only God is immortal (1 Timothy 1:17; 6:15, 16). Man is mortal by nature (Isaiah 51:12). Man's flesh is mortal (2 Corinthians 4:11). The soul is also mortal (Ezekiel 18:4). Immortality will be granted after the resurrection (1 Corinthians 15:52–55).

Christ, the hope of life. Christ promises eternal life (John 10:27, 28). Christ removes death (2 Timothy 1:10). Jesus has the keys to hell and death (Revelation 1:18).

Life and death

"If a man die, shall he live again?" (Job 14:14). This is the question that worries humanity the most. Fortunately, God in His love has expanded on the answer in His holy Word. He explains to us that life is the association of two elements: dust and breath of life (spirit) from God (Genesis 2:7). Death is the inverse process: the dust returns to the earth, and the breath of life, or vital principle given by God, returns to God (Ecclesiastes 12:7). The real cause of death is sin (Romans 6:23). Sin has passed to all men, and because of that, all must die (Romans 5:12).

Where do the dead go?

According to the Bible, the dead go to the tomb, where they sleep until the return of our Lord Jesus Christ. The word *hell* simply means "tomb," but it is not a place of perpetual suffering. The Bible does not mention purgatory. It also doesn't say that the dead go to heaven because the reward will be given to the righteous when our Lord Jesus returns and the resurrection takes place.

Can we communicate with the dead?

In desperation, many try to communicate with their dead loved ones. However, the Bible clearly teaches that the dead know nothing (Ecclesiastes 9:5, 6). Therefore, they cannot communicate with us, nor can we with them.

We must remember that Satan's first lie dealt with this matter. God told Adam that if he sinned, he would die, but Satan replied, "You shall not die" (Genesis 3:4). Satan keeps trying to deceive us in regard to death, and he is determined to maintain his original lie. He can transform "into an angel of light" (2 Corinthians 11:14). Even the demons are able to impersonate people who have died (2 Corinthians 11:15). Many of the "unexplainable" or paranormal phenomena are provoked by "spirits of devils, working miracles" (Revelation 16:14). That's why we are urged: "Believe not every spirit, but try the spirits whether they are of God" (1 John 4:1). God strictly condemns any occultist or spiritualistic practice (Leviticus 19:31; 20:27; Isaiah 8:19).

Wonderful hope

- Death is sleep. Just as sleep restores us after a hard day of work, God grants us a deserved rest after a long life filled with work (John 11:11–14).
- The resurrection. Death is not the end of everything. The farewell to the loved one is not definitive; it is simply "see you later." The Bible speaks of the blessed hope of the resurrection (Isaiah 26:19; 1 Thessalonians 4:16; John 6:40).
- The transformation. At the resurrection, the saved will have new bodies, minds, and hearts (1 Corinthians 15:42–44, 51–56; Philippians 3:20, 21).
- No more death. Just as it is with all tragedies caused by sin, God will eliminate death forever. When we reunite with our loved ones, we will do so with the total certainty that we will never again say goodbye and that there will never be separation (Isaiah 25:8; Luke 20:36).

This hope must strengthen our faith in God's promises. When a loved one dies, we will have natural human sadness, but we will have hope to dry our tears (Proverbs 14:32).

What the Bible Teaches About

THE DIVINE PLAN FOR SUPPORTING THE CHURCH

20

EVERYTHING BELONGS TO GOD

1. To whom does the universe belong? Psalm 24:1

___

2. What enormous riches does God possess? Haggai 2:8

___

3. Thanks to whom do we obtain our things? Deuteronomy 8:17, 18

___

GOD'S PART

4. What proportion of our income belongs to God? Leviticus 27:30, 32

___

5. We must give a tithe of what? Genesis 28:20–22

___

6. What is tithe used for? 1 Corinthians 9:13, 14

___

7. What wonderful blessing does God promise? Malachi 3:10

___

WHAT MUST I DO?

1. Be a faithful administrator of God's goods (1 Peter 4:10).
2. Be generous (Proverbs 11:24, 25).
3. Give cheerfully (2 Corinthians 9:6, 7).

I want to be God's partner. I promise to give cheerfully what belongs to God.

___

SIGNATURE

ADDITIONAL STUDY

God owns everything. He is the owner of heaven and earth (Deuteronomy 10:14). Animals belong to Him (Psalm 50:10–12). All wealth is His (Haggai 2:8). Our bodies and lives belong to Him (1 Corinthians 6:20).

We are God's stewards. The Lord wants us to act as His stewards (Matthew 25:14–30; Psalm 8:4–8). He gives us the strength to accumulate wealth (Deuteronomy 8:18; Proverbs 10:22), but He urges us to not love money (1 Timothy 6:10). We must be faithful stewards (1 Corinthians 4:1, 2). We must give according to the blessings God has granted us (Deuteronomy 16:17). Whatever we treasure, that is where our heart will be (Luke 12:33, 34).

Collaborators with God

The Maker is also the great Provider. He gives us life, sustenance, and knowledge of the truth. As a demonstration of His love, He makes us His collaborators. God asks the tithe of us not because He needs it but for us to remember our dependence on Him and in order to establish a beneficial partnership for us.

Tithe

Tithe is one-tenth of our earnings, and it belongs to God (Leviticus 27:30; 1 Chronicles 29:12, 14). Abraham gave his tithe to God (Genesis 14:20; Hebrews 7:1–7). Jacob also gave it (Genesis 28:22). It was a habitual practice of the Hebrew people (2 Chronicles 31:5, 6; Nehemiah 10:37, 38). Our Lord Jesus Christ approved of this practice (Matthew 23:23).

"The special system of tithing was founded upon a principle which is as enduring as the law of God. This system of tithing was a blessing to the Jews, else God would not have given it them. So also will it be a blessing to those who carry it out to the end of time."[34]

The use of tithe

Tithe was always used for sustaining worship and the ministers (Numbers 18:21). The Bible teaching is very clear that the ministers must be supported financially in order to dedicate themselves exclusively to ministry (1 Corinthians 9:13, 14; Luke 10:7). The Adventist Church uses the tithe to support the ministers who preach the gospel. This way, every cent is used directly in God's work. A chain of salvation is formed: Each of us learned the truth because others were faithful in giving tithe; now, we give so that others can have the same blessed privilege.

Other offerings

Tithe is what we return to God because it belongs to Him. Our generosity is measured by the offerings that we give voluntarily. Offerings are used for extending the gospel in our territory and in foreign missions, for the expenses of our own local church, and for special projects. The holy Bible recommends that we be generous in giving our offerings (1 Chronicles 16:29; Psalm 96:8, Mark 12:41–44).

God's marvelous promises

God promises us a partnership in the system of tithes and offerings. He, who owns all wealth, invites us to participate in the huge blessings that He pours out. That is why He asks that we give abundantly and cheerfully (2 Corinthians 9:6, 7). He promises to take care of us at every moment (Hebrews 13:5, 6). He assures us that we can try Him in His promise to grant us overabundant blessings (Malachi 3:10, 11; Proverbs 11:24, 25).

What the Bible Teaches About

THE GIFT OF PROPHECY IN THE TRUE CHURCH

21

THE PROPHETIC GIFT

1. To whom does God reveal His plans? Amos 3:7

   ____

2. How does God communicate with the prophet? Numbers 12:6

   ____

3. Can a woman be a prophet? Joel 2:28

   ____

THE PROPHETIC GIFT IN THE TRUE CHURCH

4. Did the early church have prophets? 1 Corinthians 12:28

   ____

5. What was predicted about the gift of prophecy in the true church? Revelation 12:17; 19:10

   ____

6. The promise of the gift of prophecy was fulfilled in the Adventist Church through Ellen G. White (see commentary).

   ____

WHAT MUST I DO?

1. Appreciate the prophecies (1 Thessalonians 5:20).
2. Be alert to the prophecies (2 Peter 1:19).
3. Believe in the prophets (2 Chronicles 20:20).

I accept the wonderful gift of prophecy given by God to His church.

____

SIGNATURE

ADDITIONAL STUDY

The Gift of Prophecy. The prophet is chosen by God (Deuteronomy 18:15). He/she speaks God's words (Deuteronomy 18:18) and receives revelations through dreams and visions (Joel 2:28; Job 33:14–16; Psalm 89:19; Ezekiel 1:1). The visions go together with significant physical phenomenon:

- Loss of strength (Daniel 10:8, 17).
- Unconsciousness (Daniel 10:9).
- Absence of breathing (Daniel 10:17).
- Eyes stay open (Numbers 24:3, 4).
- Receives superhuman strength (Daniel 10:18).

The Gift of Prophecy in women. The gift of prophecy was granted to many noble women: Miriam (Exodus 15:20), Deborah (Judges 4:4), Huldah (2 Kings 22:14), Noadiah (Nehemiah 6:14), Anna (Luke 2:36), and Philip's four daughters (Acts 21:8, 9).

Tests of the true prophet

A prophet: (1) speaks according to the law and the testimony (Isaiah 8:20); (2) predictions come true (Jeremiah 28:9); (3) does not lead the people into apostasy (Deuteronomy 13:1–3), (4) states what is inspired and does not speak about himself or herself (Jeremiah 14:14); (5) rebukes sin (Jeremiah 23:22).

Ellen G. White: life and work

The Adventist Church had the Spirit of Prophecy in the person of Ellen G. White. She was born in Gorham, Maine, on November 26, 1827. At twelve years old, she gave her heart to God and was baptized by a Methodist minister. With several members of her family, Ellen attended some Adventist meetings in Portland, Oregon, and in 1842, she fully accepted the doctrines. In 1843, she was disfellowshipped from the Methodist church.

As she prayed with others in December 1844, she had her first vision, in which she saw the journey of the Adventist people to God's city. She shared her vision with the believers in Portland, and they accepted it as light from God. Then she went on several trips to tell about this and other visions and to fight against fanatical movements that were creeping in among the believers.

In a trip to Orrington, Maine, she met a young Adventist preacher, James White, whom she married in August 1846. They carefully studied a pamphlet from Pastor Joseph Bates called "The Seventh Day Sabbath, a Perpetual Sign." They accepted the Sabbath, and on April 7, 1847, she received a vision in which she saw God's law with a light that shown over the fourth commandment.

The visions

Thousands of people saw Ellen White in vision. The same phenomena described in the Bible regarding the ancient prophets manifested in her. During one of her visions, she took a heavy Bible weighing almost twenty pounds and held it at arm's length for half an hour; when strong men tried to do the same thing, they were only able to do so for a few minutes. In her visions she was transported to other countries, which she later recognized in her trips.

One of her most important visions was about the great controversy between good and evil. That vision happened in March 1858 in Ohio. Another vision was about health. As a result of that vision, the church started to emphasize temperance and medical work. She had almost two thousand dreams and visions with revelations about all aspects of the truth and the organization of the church.

Missionary

Along with her husband, Ellen White traveled extensively throughout the United States preaching and helping in the organization of the church, and fighting against problems and errors. She went to Europe in the fall of 1885. In 1891, she went to Australia, where she helped to strengthen and establish the work on that continent.

Author

White wrote thousands of pages and about forty-five books. Some of her best-known books are *Steps to Christ*, *The Great Controversy*, *The Desire of Ages*, *Patriarchs and Prophets*, *Education*, and *Ministry of Healing*.

What the Bible Teaches About

PERSONAL SURRENDER TO GOD

22

NECESSARY CONDITION

1. What step is essential for salvation? Mark 16:16

____

GOD'S TENDER INVITATIONS

2. What calling did Jesus make to Levi? Luke 5:27

____

3. How did Levi respond? Luke 5:28

____

4. What other gentle calling does Jesus make? Revelation 3:20

____

5. What decision must we make now? Acts 22:16

____

WHAT MUST I DO?

1. Do not postpone the decision to accept the Lord (Acts 24:25).
2. Together with your family, make a decision for God (Joshua 24:15).
3. Make the decision right now (Hebrews 3:15).
4. Ask for baptism (Acts 8:36).
5. Trust fully in Jesus (Philippians 4:13).

I believe that the Lord calls me to join His church. I respond joyfully to His calling, and I surrender my life through baptism.

____

SIGNATURE

COMMITMENT TO GOD

"I can do all things through Christ which strengtheneth me."—Philippians 4:13

BY GOD'S GRACE I PROMISE:

1. To accept Jesus as my only Savior (Acts 4:12).
2. To abandon sin, having obtained forgiveness that God offers for repentance, confession, and conversion (1 John 1:9).
3. To accept the Bible as the only rule of faith. To study it daily through the Sabbath School lessons (John 5:39).
4. To pray three times a day (Daniel 6:10).
5. To faithfully observe, by God's grace, His holy commandments (James 2:10).
6. To rest on the holy Sabbath. Not to carry out any work on the Sabbath. To attend worship services (Exodus 20:8–11).
7. To accept the Spirit of Prophecy (2 Chronicles 20:20).
8. To live in a healthful way. To abstain from unsuitable meats, alcoholic beverages, and every vice (1 Corinthians 6:19, 20).
9. To dress with Christian modesty (1 Timothy 2:9).
10. To cooperate with God in the tithing and offerings plan (Malachi 3:6–9).
11. To use my talents to serve God as a volunteer missionary, winning souls for Christ (Luke 8:38, 39).
12. To accept the guidance of the church and its pastors. (Hebrews 13:17).

BY GOD'S GRACE, I DECLARE:

1. To know, accept, and practice Jesus' doctrine.
2. That I request to be baptized by immersion. I ask to be accepted as a member of the Seventh-day Adventist Church.

Name ____________________

Address ____________________

Signature ____________________

Instructor ____________________

You will be baptized at ____________________

On this date and time ____________________

EDUCATION FOR ETERNITY 23

EDUCATING OUR CHILDREN

1. What advice is given to parents about the education of their children? Deuteronomy 6:5–9

____

2. What is the biblical precedent for church schools? 2 Kings 6:1–7

____

CHRIST'S SCHOOL

3. What was the fundamental task carried out by the Lord Jesus? Matthew 4:23

____

SCHOOLS TODAY

4. What dangers do Christians face in non-Christian schools or colleges? 1 Timothy 6:20, 21

____

OBJECTIVES OF CHRISTIAN EDUCATION

5. What are the Lord's objectives for His children? Isaiah 54:13

____

WHAT MUST I DO?

1. Instruct our children in the Lord (Proverbs 22:6).
2. Accept God's command (Deuteronomy 6:6).
3. Allow our children to go to Jesus (Matthew 19:14).

I will do whatever is in my reach to help the children and youth be taught by the Lord.

____

SIGNATURE

ADDITIONAL STUDY

Education: Is it biblical?

The concepts studied reveal to us that the education of our children deserves serious consideration and a definite effort so that they can follow heaven's principles and reach salvation.

"To restore in man the image of his Maker, to bring him back to the perfection in which he was created, to promote the development of body, mind, and soul, that the divine purpose in his creation might be realized—this was to be the work of redemption. This is the object of education, the great object of life."[35]

Education and redemption join together; they are mixed in the effort to take man toward a relationship with God that is as similar as possible to that other existence, before sin, as well as a perfect relationship in the coming world.

In its work of education, the world strives only to develop natural powers. It omits restoration, which is the more important of the two processes. No education that omits the work of restoration can be called Christian. A child who studies in a school where spiritual restoration is not cared for cannot say he or she is being "taught of the Lord." However, the Bible says: "All thy children shall be taught of the LORD" (Isaiah 54:13).

Elementary school

"Even so it is not the will of your father which is in heaven, that one of these little ones should perish" (Matthew 18:14).

"Children are a heritage from the Lord, and they are to be trained for His service. This is the work that rests upon parents and teachers with solemn, sacred force, which they cannot evade or ignore. To neglect this work marks them as unfaithful servants; but there is a reward when the seed of truth is early sown in the heart and carefully tended."[36]

High schools and colleges

The divine purpose for education covers not just elementary education but all levels. Secondary and college education have a triple objective:

1. To continue with the work of restoration and redemption.
2. To serve as cities of refuge against the tide of evil that is ever-increasing.
3. To prepare young people for service to the Lord.

In these days in which the church is growing very rapidly, we need to preserve the most precious thing she possesses—the children and the youth—from the demoralizing influences and prevailing immorality in the world.

Expense or investment

What a wonderful attitude toward education would be developed if all of us—parents, grandparents, members of the church—could look at the money that we pay for the education of our children and youth as an investment instead of an expense!

Psalm 127:3 says: "Children are an heritage of the LORD." What a beautiful truth! Children are a gift from the Lord, and we must celebrate this blessing.

The Adventist Church has recognized, from its beginning, the value of Christian education for their children. Great sacrifices are made in order for the youth of the church to obtain an Adventist education. Parents sacrifice even things that are essential for life as long as they can send their children to Adventist schools.

Also, the church has invested millions of dollars in the educational system.

What shall we do?

"The Lord of heaven is looking on to see who is doing the work He would have done for the children and youth. . . .

"As a church, as individuals, if we would stand clear in the judgment, we must make more liberal efforts for the training of our young people."[37]

Suggested for further study

White: *Education, Christian Education, Counsels for Teachers, Child Guidance*

THE FUTURE REVEALED 24

GOD REVEALS THE FUTURE

1. Who alone knows the future? Isaiah 46:9, 10

 ____

2. To whom does God entrust His plans? Amos 3:7

 ____

3. What do the prophecies resemble? 2 Peter 1:19

 ____

REVEALING THE FUTURE OF THE NATIONS

4. Who was Daniel? Daniel 1:6, 8, 17, 20

 ____

5. What strange dream did Nebuchadnezzar have? Daniel 2:31–35

 ____

6. What nations were represented by the great image? Daniel 2:36–40

 ____

- **Head of gold:** Babylon, 605–538 B.C.
- **Chest and arms of silver:** Media-Persia, 538–331 B.C.
- **Belly and thighs of bronze:** Greece, 331–168 B.C.
- **Legs of iron:** Rome, 168 B.C.–A.D. 476

7. What would happen when Rome fell? Daniel 2:41–43

 ____

8. Would a new universal kingdom rise up? Daniel 2:44

 ____

A NEW WORLD

9. Who will establish a new kingdom? Daniel 2:44, 45

 ____

10. What characteristics will the new world have? Revelation 21:1–4

 ____

I believe in the prophecies. I want to prepare myself to live in God's new kingdom.

____

SIGNATURE

THE MOST EXTRAORDINARY PROPHECY

25

Note: Daniel chapters 8 and 9 present an extraordinary prophecy, and its development covers 2,300 years. The first part refers to the Hebrew people and to the coming of the Messiah. The last part has a direct relationship with the marvelous events related to the history of God's people.

1. What great events were foretold?

____

2. During how much time would these events take place? Daniel 8:12

____

3. When did the long period of 2,300 years begin? Daniel 8:13, 14

____

Note: Artaxerxes, king of Persia, issued the decree in 457 B.C.

THE COMING OF THE MESSIAH

4. What portion of the 2,300 years was for the Jews? Daniel 9:25

____

5. When did the Messiah appear? Daniel 9:24

____

Note: Seven weeks plus sixty-two weeks equals sixty-nine weeks; 483 prophetic days (literal years). Starting in the year 457 B.C., this takes us to the year A.D. 27, when Jesus was baptized.

6. How is the death of the Messiah foretold? Daniel 9:25, 26

____

A WORK OF JUDGMENT AND RESTORATION

7. What anxious question did the prophet ask? Daniel 8:13

____

8. When would the great prophetic period come to an end? Daniel 8:14

____

Note: Starting in 457 B.C., the prophetic period would end in 1844.

9. What would happen on that date? Daniel 8:14

____

- The investigative judgment would start.
- The eternal truths would be restored.

I thank God for the revelation of the future that is expressed in His Word.

____

SIGNATURE

ONE THOUSAND YEARS OF PEACE

26

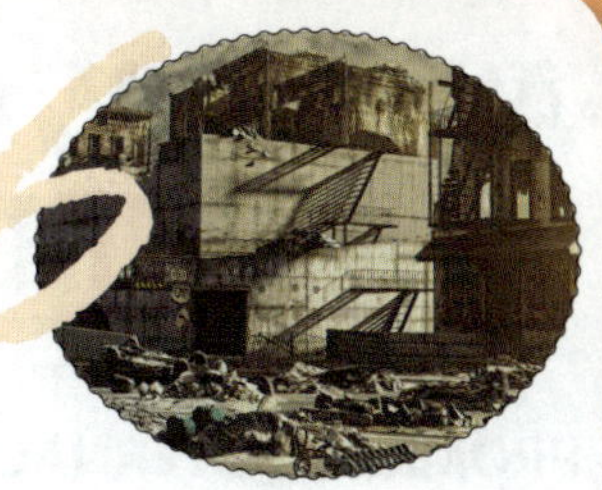

Note: Immediately after the second coming of Jesus, a period called the millennium (one thousand years) begins. The redeemed will go with Jesus to God's dwelling, where they will reign and judge the wicked. It ends with the third coming of Christ to earth, the final destruction of the wicked, and the definitive establishment of Jesus' kingdom on earth.

THE BEGINNING OF THE MILLENNIUM

1. With what event does the millennium begin? 1 Thessalonians 4:15–17

   ____

2. What will happen with the righteous dead and living? 1 Thessalonians 4:16, 17

   ____

3. What will happen with the wicked? 1 Corinthians 15:51, 52; 2 Thessalonians 2:8–12

   ____

DURING THE MILLENNIUM

4. What will happen to Satan? Revelation 20:1–3; Jeremiah 4:23–27

   ____

Note: The saints remain with Jesus in God's dwelling, where they reign and judge the wicked. During that time, the earth remains desolate and void. Because Satan has no one to deceive, he is bound by the circumstances.

THE END OF THE MILLENNIUM

5. What event marks the end of the millennium? Revelation 21:2, 3

   ____

6. What happens with Satan and the wicked? Revelation 20:5, 7–9

   ____

7. What is the end of Satan and the wicked? Revelation 20:10

   ____

8. Will sin rise up again? Malachi 4:1

   ____

I will live as a committed Christian to reign with Jesus for eternity.

____

SIGNATURE

A NEW WORLD OF HAPPINESS

27

PROMISE OF ETERNAL HAPPINESS

1. What will be the final reward for all who believe in Jesus? John 3:16

___

2. What has God prepared for those who love Him? 1 Corinthians 2:9

___

GLIMPSES OF THE NEW EARTH

3. What will disappear in the new earth? Revelation 21:3, 4

___

4. How is the new earth described? Isaiah 65:21–25

___

5. Who will dwell with the redeemed? Revelation 21:3

___

6. How long will the new kingdom last? Revelation 22:1–5

___

CITIZENS OF THE ETERNAL KINGDOM

7. Who will enter in the kingdom? Matthew 7:21

___

8. What condition will be indispensable? Revelation 22:14

___

9. What is the passport to enter the kingdom? Isaiah 26:2

___

10. What counsel is given to those who wish to go to heaven? 1 John 3:2, 3

___

I will prepare to be a citizen of Jesus' eternal kingdom.

___

SIGNATURE

THE CHRISTIAN HOME 28

THE INSTITUTION OF MARRIAGE

1. Who instituted marriage, and when did He do so? Genesis 1:28; 2:18

2. What did Jesus say about marriage? Matthew 19:5, 6

COUNSEL FOR A HAPPY MARRIAGE

3. Who is the head of the home? Ephesians 5:22, 23

4. What qualities must the wife have? Titus 2:4, 5

5. What flaw must the wife avoid? Proverbs 21:9, 19

6. What excellent description is given of a wife and mother? Proverbs 31:19–31

7. What instruction is given to husbands? Colossians 3:19

8. What must be the main quality of the husband? Ephesians 5:28, 29

EDUCATION OF CHILDREN

9. What is the main duty of parents? Proverbs 22:6

10. What is the recommendation about punishment? Proverbs 13:24

11. What error must be avoided in education? Ephesians 6:4

12. What is the essential teaching? 2 Timothy 3:15–17

13. What is the main thing in the education of children? Isaiah 54:13

I will strive to honor God in my home. I will be a good spouse and a wise and loving parent.

SIGNATURE

THE STRUGGLES OF THE CHRISTIAN 29

THERE WILL BE TRIALS

1. Who is the enemy, and what does he try to do? 1 Peter 5:8

____

2. What problems can we expect? Matthew 10:21, 22

____

3. What guarantee does God give us? 1 Corinthians 10:13

____

STRUGGLING WITH THE TRIALS

4. What must we avoid when facing trials? 2 Corinthians 4:16, 17

____

5. What is the source of victory? 2 Corinthians 12:9, 10

____

6. What weapon is quick and powerful? Hebrews 4:12

____

7. What will help us win the battle? 1 Timothy 6:11, 12

____

8. What other victorious weapon do we have? James 5:16

____

9. What powerful weapons does the Christian have? Ephesians 6:11–18

____

PROMISES OF VICTORY

10. What is the secret to overcome Satan? James 4:7

____

11. What certainty do those who love God have? Romans 8:28

____

12. What will be the reward for those who fight? 2 Timothy 4:7, 8

____

I will fight with courage, sure of victory in Christ.

____

SIGNATURE

DUTIES AND PRIVILEGES OF THE CHURCH MEMBER

30

PRIVILEGES OF THE CHURCH MEMBER

1. The faithful church member is a child of whom? 1 John 3:1–3

   ____

2. What does the child of God inherit? Galatians 4:5–7

   ____

DUTIES OF THE CHURCH MEMBER

3. What is God's instruction regarding worship and church attendance? Hebrews 10:25

   ____

4. What recommendation does God give us regarding His Word? Deuteronomy 17:19

   ____

5. What must our commitment be regarding the preaching of the gospel? Matthew 24:14

   ____

6. How must we exercise our faith? Hebrews 10:23

   ____

7. What is our responsibility to the world? Matthew 5:13, 14

   ____

8. What should be our relationship with pastors? 1 Thessalonians 5:12, 13

   ____

9. What challenge does God present to us about supporting the work? Malachi 3:10

   ____

10. How should we relate with brothers and sisters in the faith? Colossians 3:13–15

    ____

11. What is the main duty of the Christian? 1 John 4:20, 21

    ____

I want God to use me; I want to be a good church member and disciple of the Lord Jesus.

____

SIGNATURE

TEN KEYS FOR OBTAINING VICTORY

31

1. Accept the whole truth and walk in all the light you have received (1 John 1:7; Proverbs 23:23).
2. Remain united with Christ (John 15:4, 5).
3. Read your Bible every day (Acts 17:11).
4. Pray to God at least three times a day (Daniel 6:10).
5. Attend meetings at church; above all, attend meetings that are held on the Sabbath (Luke 4:16; Acts 10:25).
6. Trust fully in God (Psalm 91:1–16).
7. If you fall in sin, seek Jesus. He is your Savior; confess your sins to Him (Acts 4:12; 1 John 2:1).
8. Prepare yourself for the second coming of Christ (1 John 3:2, 3).
9. Be a disciple of Jesus and share your faith (Acts 1:8).
10. Grow in holiness (Hebrews 12:14; Proverbs 4:18).

With God's help, I will strive to be faithful until the end (Revelation 2:10).

____

SIGNATURE

Endnotes

1. Walter M. Abbott and Joseph Gallagher, ed., *The Documents of Vatican II* (New York: American Press, 1966), 125, 127.

2. Andrew Conway Ivy, "The Absoluteness of the Certainty of God's Existence," in *The Evidence of God in an Expanding Universe: Forty American Scientist Declare Their Affirmative Views on Religion,* ed. John Clover Monsma (New York: Putnam, 1958).

3. Will Durant, *On the Meaning of Life* (New York: Ray Long and Richard Smith, 1932).

4. Isaac Newton, *The Mathematical Principles of Natural Philosophy* London: 1729), 388.

5. Werhner von Braun, "Why I Believe: Werhner von Braun Talks About Science and God," *National Sunday Magazine for a Better America,* July 18, 1965.

6. Ellen G. White, "The Father, Son, and Holy Ghost," *Bible Training School,* March 1, 1906.

7. White, "The Father, Son, and Holy Ghost."

8. LeRoy Edwin Froom, *The Coming of the Comforter* (Washington, DC: Review and Herald®, 1928), 40.

9. Ellen G. White, *Steps to Christ* (Washington, DC: Review and Herald®, 1956), 93, 94.

10. Alexis Carrel, "Prayer Is Power," *Reader's Digest,* March 1941.

11. White, *Steps to Christ,* 100.

12. *Catechism of Christian Doctrine* (Charlotte, NC: St. Benedict, 2012) 141.

13. Abbott and Gallagher, *Vatican II,* 80.

14. Billy Graham, *World Aflame* (New York: Doubleday, 1965), 194.

15. *Bible Readings for the Home Circle* (Battle Creek, MI: Review and Herald®, 1889)

16. Graham, *World Aflame,* 224, 225.

17. Abbott and Gallagher, *Vatican II,* 67.

18. White, *Steps to Christ,* 21.

19. White, *Steps to Christ,* 38, 39.

20. White, *Steps to Christ,* 58.

21. Graham, *World Aflame,* 167.

22. White, *Steps to Christ,* 69, 70.

23. Abbott and Gallagher, *Vatican II,* 214, 215.

24. P. A. Hillaire, *La Religion Demostrada o Los fundamentos de la fe católica ante la razón y la ciencia* (Barcelona: Luis Gili, 1944), 500, translated by author.

25. Hillaire, *Demostrada,* 508.

26. Charles Buck, *Theological Dictionary* (Philadelphia, 1826), s.v. "Sabbath."

27. James Cardinal Gibbons, *The Faith of Our Fathers* (Baltimore, 1898), 111, 112.

28. Bruce W. Frier, ed. *The Codex of Justinian,* vol. 3, Third Book, 12.2, trans. Justice Fred H. Blume (Cambridge: Cambridge University Press, 2016), 643.

29. Augustus Neander, *General History of the Christian Religion and Church,* vol. 1, 1st German ed., trans. H. J. Rose (London, 1841), 186.

30. Ellen G. White, "Words to the Young," *The Youth's Instructor,* May 4, 1893.

31. Gibbons, *Faith of Our Fathers,* 317.

32. *Nuevo Trestamento,* trans. Juan Straubinger (1969), 614.

33. Ellen G. White, *Counsels on Health* (Mountain View, CA: Pacific Press®, 1951), 41.

34. Ellen G. White, *Testimonies for the Church,* vol. 3 (Mountain View, CA: Pacific Press®, 1948), 404.

35. Ellen G. White, *Education* (Nampa, ID: Pacific Press®, 2002), 15, 16.

36. Ellen G. White, *Counsels to Parents, Teachers, and Students* (Mountain View, CA: Pacific Press®, 1913), 143, 144.

37. White, *Counsels to Parents,* 42, 43.

NOTES

NOTES

NOTES